Who Should I Be Today?

Jaylene English

Unless otherwise indicated, Bible quotations are taken from the Amplified Bible, copyright © 1987 by The Lockman Foundation; the New King James Version, copyright © 1982 by Thomas Nelson, Inc.; the Holy Bible, New International Version, copyright © 1973, 1978, 1984 by Zondervan; and the Holy Bible, New Living Translation, copyright © 1996, 2004, by Tyndale House Publishers, Inc.

ACKNOWLEDGEMENTS

How do you say thank you for a new chance at life that you know you don't deserve? I don't know either! But I do know that I have tried to thank God repeatedly and it never seems like the words "thank you" are enough. So I try my best to "live a lifestyle of thankfulness" each day.

These are people in my life who I want to thank for help with writing this book:

To my husband, Mike, who "pushed and pushed" for several years, along with Kim & Butch Stanger, to get me to write this book. They continuously encouraged me to write it for those who are alone and hurting, who need to believe that with God all things are possible. They each have loved me unconditionally, through good, bad and ugly; they've never stopped believing in me.

Pastor Randy & Cindy McAllister, who believed in me, and saw what God has done and is continuing to do in my life, that there is a purpose for my life. They truly showed me that even a life like mine is one to be celebrated and not just tolerated.

To Amy who allowed me to mentor her, and in the process she "chose to believe" and take it to the next step, applying changes to her life. She is a true gift from God and will always be a reminder of why I go forward each day to reach out to others who the **world views as hopeless**. Don't ever stop believing.

To Michelle Schroeder for all of her hours of work editing this book, and encouraging me through the entire process of writing and publishing it. But even more so for not judging my past, just seeing me for who I am today. You are priceless.

To Pastor Will & Teresa who loved us unconditionally through everything. They said "yes" to reaching out to me, and to being those parents who helped me to grow, heal, and learn to live for the first time. I love you both so much.

To my children who have given me a second chance at being their mom. I love them all so much. I can never change what I've done, but I can change who I am each day for the future.

My husband Mike... you are my best friend, thank you for simply loving me.

PREFACE

In September 1958 at San Francisco General Hospital, a baby girl was born. But her arrival in this world was not celebrated - she was not wanted or planned. She was an intrusion to her family.

Before she could even talk, she was being used to sexually satisfy adult men all around her. Because of the continuous molestation, her body was already trained in masturbation as a toddler. She used the crib rails, at times so intensely she physically harmed herself. The adults in her life simply watched in amusement.

The night of her brother's birth, when she was 16 months old, the abuse was so intense she began convulsing. But her mother showed no concern for her wellbeing. Instead she was annoyed to be distracted during her labor.

Her family moved when she was almost four. But the abuse didn't stop - new men entered her life, family friends and relatives. By the age of five she had been with more men than most adult women. But this was normal to her. It was all she knew. This was how she was being trained to love.

****

1963

Here he comes. I can hear his footsteps coming down the stairs... which one is it? I need to know who to be. The voices tell me to listen closely to the steps. I close my eyes and can tell from the sound. Hurry and change. He's closer now. My heart is beating so loud and fast. I must remember who I am supposed to be. What things do I do this time?

The footsteps stop. I know he's making sure the other children are asleep. It's what they all do before coming in. The figure is there in the doorway, and I know who I am to be. I've memorized the things he wants me to do. Don't cry, don't cry, don't cry... I remind myself it only hurts for a little while. I'm so scared. What if I do it wrong? Will it hurt more this time? What if I throw up? My heart's too loud - he'll know I'm scared. If I pretend I'm asleep maybe he'll go away. Then the first touch, and my body and the voices take over.

The voices are helping me to remember. *Smile. Look at him. Make him happy. He needs you to help him. He loves you so much, little girl, because you're extra special. You make him feel good.* Help me, somebody please help me! It hurts and I can't stop my body. Please take me away.

There are the voices again. *Who will help you, little girl? Look at him, see how much he wants you; he's helping you now to feel good. He loves you. Can't you feel his love? Just wait and see, he'll hold you and make it all better.*

Now he's saying all that yucky stuff. I hate it when they talk. "Okay, honey, open your mouth." My head is screaming no, but I do what I'm told. Soon it's over, and he picks me up and puts me in his lap. "I love you, Jaylene. You're so pretty, so good and special." Then he's gone.

I crawl to my closet and curl up in a tight ball so no one can hear me cry. I look up and see my pretty new dress hanging there. Soon I will start kindergarten and that will be a good day. I feel sick and dirty. I need to get clean. I hope there are no others tonight.

CHAPTER 1

Growing up, I lived in a small town on the Columbia River. I mostly remember it as a place for me to just survive, but I also liked to explore. I would go climbing in the hills, making-believe I was a different person with a different life, and I was on an adventure.

In make-believe, I could recreate my life as something good... I belonged to a family, and I looked like I fit in with them. I was beautiful, clean and safe. I had a mom who loved me and wanted me. But at the end of each make-believe adventure, reality was waiting for me at home, where I was dirty, ugly, and unwanted – except by the men.

I always knew my mom didn't like me very much. I didn't look right; I didn't look like anyone else in the family. My grandmas would tell me that too, "You're so different, Jaylene." I knew that if I could be like the other little girls, my mom would be happier.

Every morning before school I whined and begged my mom not to do my hair. She pulled the comb through my hair, and then yelled at me to stand still while she combed it out all over again. Next she would rat my hair with the comb and use lots of hairspray to give me a beehive hairdo. I hated having hair that looked like the big girls'.

I remember how scared I felt on my first day of kindergarten. How would I know what to do?

What if I didn't do things right? When it was time to go, I picked up my lunch box that looked like a barn. We got to the school, and my mom told me to hurry because I was late - everyone else was already inside. "Please don't make me go!" I cried. "Stop crying and get in there," she yelled.

I got out of the car and started down the little hill to the school when the wind caught my hair and blew it straight up in the air. With all of that hair spray it stood stiff. As I saw my reflection in the giant windows by the door, I looked so small. I cried out to my mom, but she just yelled at me again to quit crying and get inside. My hair wouldn't go back down, and my tears wouldn't stop. My grown-up hair was all messed up, and I knew the kids were going to laugh at me. I wanted to hide.

Then a man asked me my name, and said, "Come with me." Now I knew I would be okay. I had heard those words from lots of men. He was going to teach me something new.

But he took me to a room with lots of other children. The room was filled with bright colors and exciting things to do. I joined in with the other kids. When I heard the teacher say it was nap time, my body knew what to do. I went to my chair and started the moving. It was stronger today.

"Stop that!" Who was yelling? I knew I must go faster and harder. *Harder, little girl, harder – you can't stop now.*

"Stop that now, Jaylene! What is the matter with you?" the teacher yelled. I started crying. I knew I didn't do the moving good enough for her. She didn't like me; she looked mean now.

Then I heard my voices again: *Come on, little girl, you know how to do this. Start over, but you must push hard.* I always did what the voices said. They were my friends. I got scared when they left me because I didn't know what to do. I started over.

"I told you to stop that nasty thing! You come with me right now!" Why was she pulling me away? I couldn't stop now – my body wouldn't like it. *No!* I felt my body jerking – I hadn't finished. It was hard to breathe now. Where was she taking me? *Stop, I have to finish!* Didn't she know I wasn't finished? Then I heard laughter. All the kids were laughing at me.

Each day at school was the same. I tried to stop, tried not to do that thing the teacher said was nasty, but I couldn't stop. Sometimes she moved me away from the other kids and away from any furniture. I just kept trying to do better. I knew that if I did what my voices said, and if I did it good enough, people wouldn't be upset with me, and the laughing would stop.

CHAPTER 2

My favorite place to be was my grandparent's farm on the Indian Reservation. It was surrounded by pine-covered mountains and lots of animals. It was quiet, peaceful and safe, like a fortress. I always felt safe when I stayed with them there. It was the most beautiful place I'd ever seen.

But Grandpa was always mean to Grandma. Sometimes he took her away to the hospital. Mom said it was his vacation time - they gave him money because Grandma's mind was not right. He had girlfriends he visited for a while, and then he would bring Grandma home again. He needed her to work the farm.

One day my dad told me that the farm had been sold because Grandpa was not well anymore. Now from early spring to late fall they lived on an old homestead place in the canyon where my grandfather's family lived when he was a child. It was my new favorite place, but I missed the farm with its mountains and trees.

On the homestead there was no electricity or indoor plumbing. A spring was just behind the little two-room house, and when I visited we slept on feather mattresses on the floor along the wall. I loved it when Grandma read to us. The light from the kerosene lamp glowed softly in the room, making me feel so cozy. I loved her; she was always strong. I didn't think she had a sick mind.

In the mornings I gathered eggs, worked in the garden and fetched water. I helped my grandmother with laundry, trying hard to scrub as well as her on the washboard. On sunny days my favorite thing was walking barefoot in the dirt. It felt so warm and soft on my feet. Often that walking led me to a fishing hole, and I always hoped I could bring home a good catch for dinner.

I loved staying with my grandparents, but those visits were usually short. At home in town, our family life bustled with lots of friends and family around. There was always something to celebrate with a few drinks, at least that's the way it seemed.

One particular uncle enjoyed taking us down to the top of the dam after he'd had a few too many drinks. Then he would hang my cousin and me over the side of the dam, holding us by our ankles. All I could see was the water rushing over, spraying in my face. Terror gripped me so that I couldn't even scream or cry. I could hardly breathe, always wondering if this would be the time he would really let go.

My brother, two sisters and I fought a lot, but we loved each other. We banded together to survive. Our mom preferred to be working at the restaurants, or just out someplace without us. In reality, she just didn't know how to take care of us.

Just before my sixth birthday, I was playing outside with my brother Dale and my cousin Charlie who lived just two houses down. We picked up a cigarette butt off the ground and I tried to light it

11

with a match. But the burning match fell in the lap of my dress. I watched as a big brown spot quickly grew. The boys poked it with sticks trying to put it out, but suddenly flames exploded.

The flames leapt higher and higher, and piercing screams filled my ears. I ran toward home. I saw my mother standing in the street, but she turned and ran away from me screaming. My dress was on fire, and the flames just kept growing. Then someone grabbed me and threw me to the ground, rolling me over and over in the dirt.

Finally the flames were put out, but the screams were so loud they were terrifying me. They were so loud I couldn't hear – then I realized that it was me. I had never screamed before, not even during all of the things with men that hurt. I was not supposed to scream. Now I couldn't stop.

The man who had saved me, our neighbor Stan, held me in his lap while my mom drove me to the hospital. "It hurts, it won't quit hurting!" I cried again and again. The awful smell of it made me sick.

In the emergency room they sprinkled some sort of powder over my burns. But then they had to send me home, because the doctor was gone fishing. A police officer came to our house to help prevent me from going into shock. The burns ranged from my knee to my chin, a combination of second and third degree burns. I had nightmares about the fire, and even in my dreams I could smell my burnt skin.

Finally, I was taken to another farming community where the doctor who had delivered my dad worked. He began the long, arduous process of treating my burns. An ointment was applied and then they wrapped me with gauze like a mummy. At nights they took me to the neighbors' to soak in their bathtub. Then it was time for the painful removal of the gauze. It ripped off the top layers of dead burnt tissue as it came off. Then a new application of ointment and gauze was put on the burns.

The school nurse wrote to the Shriner's, requesting treatment for me. I was accepted, and years of skin grafting began. The removal of stitches was an agonizing ordeal for everyone involved: me, those holding me down, and the doctor trying to work as I lay there screaming in pain. It was one long, circular stitch which often took up to half an hour to remove. I remember seeing sweat on Dr. Sullivan's face as he worked to pull it out - or maybe he was crying, too.

During those years of surgeries, I wasn't permitted to go outside at recess time to play with the other children. I felt isolated and alone. But Mrs. Doughty, the school secretary, took me under her wing and I began to spend time helping in the office. By second grade I was helping to type the school bulletin, run copies on the big, crank-handled copier machine, and deliver the bulletins to the classrooms.

I excelled in this area as my clerical skills grew. For the first time in my life I was commended for doing well at something. I didn't feel like a failure when I was in the office. Someone actually liked me and believed in me. I will always remember her words to me one day: "Jaylene, you're not a freak. Your life matters. You just need to focus on good things."

I couldn't be physically active because of the surgeries, and I began to get chubby. The kids made fun of me, especially in the summer months at the beach. Doctors insisted that I wear a two-piece swimsuit to expose the scar tissue, and children called me names like "Frankenstein's sister". When I jumped into the water they yelled "tidal wave".

Even grown-ups often stared at me. I hated seeing people gawk and whisper as I walked by. I began to hear many voices in my head, telling me there was no one who could ever accept a freak like me. I would always be alone and unloved. I was an embarrassment to my family. It was my fault that my mom's life was ruined - if I hadn't been born she would be happy and living a better life.

But the other voices told me that those were lies, because the men still loved me. And even more would love me, the nicer I was to them. I always did extra good with them now. I worked hard to be everything they wanted. I listened real well when they talked about how much they hurt, and even learned what to say and do to make them feel better. The voices took care of me. They helped me to remember what each man liked to hear. I was really good at knowing the sound of their footsteps now, and I changed faster than before so I talked and acted just right. Just like putting on a Halloween mask, I could be whatever they wanted.

CHAPTER 3

No matter where I went - to a friend's house, a relative's, the beach - there were men who wanted to love me and teach me how to take care of them. I hated this aspect of my life, but I understood that it was what I was supposed to do. This was what made me special.

One day I was invited to go on a campout with my friend's family, with her brother, sister and cousin. Her dad and uncle were taking us camping out by the lake. I packed my clothes in a little bag and waited excitedly for them to pick me up. At the lake I played happily all day long with the other kids. I was thrilled to be spending a whole day with kids, not grown-ups. But when we got ready to go to bed, I didn't get to sleep with the other kids. I was taken to bed with the two men, and they taught me new things for a long time that night.

They were so happy with me, they said, and they were always going to take care of me. It was a special secret that no one else could share. No one was as special as me, the uncle said. He never loved anyone so much. And then the dad started things again while the uncle watched. They twisted me just right, and told me how to talk. They took lots of pictures, and they smiled when they showed me how pretty I was.

Something changed in me that night. My body was doing sick things, but it didn't hurt. I couldn't feel anything. *Why?*, I wondered. *Am I*

16

dying? Will it hurt when I'm dead? I think I would like it if I could die. Why can't I cry? Where are the voices?

What happened shortly after that was even scarier. I began to molest other children. I knew how to teach them now. *I'm a big girl now*, the voices said. *I'm in third grade.*

Even in the act of being the abuser I hated it. I spent hours scrubbing myself and my room, but I could never get clean. No matter how many tears I cried they kept coming. Inside I was screaming for help, but I didn't understand how to get it, or even what it was. I told some grown-ups about things that were happening, but that didn't stop it. So what was help?

When I needed to help myself feel better, one place I could go was to a rock house that was up the road from ours. I don't remember anyone living there, but I loved that place. Something about it made me feel safe and warm inside. I didn't go in it - just looking at the rocks of the house made me think it was strong and that it would protect me.

I spent hours playing, pretending I was riding horses around the building. Sometimes I played house on the little porch. I was by myself, but I pretended I had a family and friends. Other times, when I was hurting badly in my private parts and I was extra scared, I would go there to hide - just curl up in a ball on the porch hoping that maybe no one would ever find me again.

By the time I was nine years old there were so many men. Some of them spoke to me as if I were a grown woman. They told me about their struggles in life and in their marriages. I laid there quietly, hoping it would soon be over. Often the wives of these men had me come help them at their homes with cleaning and babysitting. They too talked to me about their own struggles - fears of their husbands seeing other women, feelings of not being good enough, and their real feelings that they couldn't share with others.

Why did any of them think I could understand these things? Maybe because I never was a child, really - I had not been given that opportunity in life. I may have been nine in years, but in my mind and heart I had already experienced more than most of the women who spoke to me. I wanted to make them feel better, but I didn't know how to yet. Someday, the voices said, they'll teach me.

During that year, the pastor of the local Nazarene church picked kids up in a bus for Sunday school each week. I loved going and I desperately wanted to be there for every event. It seemed so clean, and I knew inside me that it was a safe place. But after a while that pastor was moved to another town, and the new pastor who came was different. He was busy, and I didn't fit in there anymore.

Before long, the drinks I was taking off my dad's beers were tasting better and better. I liked the numbness I felt. I discovered that pain medications helped too, and then people introduced me to even more kinds of drugs. I remember watching something on the news about a lot of people on LSD - it sounded dangerous. I told my dad, "I'm afraid of being a drug addict". He told me I wouldn't be, and I tried to believe him. I can still see that moment clearly, as we were in the car on the way to the city shop where he worked.

At the end of fourth grade, my dad and I went out one night to look for my mom. All we knew was that she was out someplace with another man. I remember exactly where we were as he was driving, when he revealed to me that he was not my real dad. I was stunned - I didn't understand. *Where do I belong? Is everything a lie?* My head was spinning. Looking up at him, I saw tears on his face, and I knew I needed to help him feel better. It was my job.

I asked him where my real dad was. He told me that he had died in a car accident when I was very young. But he also told me something special. "Your dad loved you very much. He used to take you to his house for visits." It was enough for my little mind to use as part of my make-believe times.

After that night my mom and dad separated, and my mom sent us girls to stay with our grandma for the summer. My maternal grandmother moved from place to place, mostly working as a cook at truck stops. But for several years she lived with a man who had a dairy farm in Yakima. This was where we went to stay with her.

I loved this place. Before the sun was all the way up I was out rounding up the cows, helping to milk them, cleaning out stalls, feeding and helping wean the calves, changing sprinklers in the corn fields, and helping with the household chores. It seemed that no chore was too difficult for me, and I loved every minute of it.

I was thankful to be free of the things that went on back home. But one thing I was never free of was the masturbation. Even though I hated it, my body craved it. It had complete control over my life. I had learned the importance of hiding and doing things in secret. The sick, dirty feeling after each act, the shame and embarrassment, and the feeling of being controlled by something I couldn't even see, was more frightening than the things I could see.

It was a summer of hard work, but the time I got to spend on the horses was well worth it. A beautiful dark thoroughbred quarter mix named Zar was my horse when I was there. Riding on Zar was heavenly. I dreamed that one day I would ride away on him and never come back to the pain.

Late that summer my mom called our grandma telling her to put us girls on the train to Spokane. Grandma bought us matching outfits for the trip, with bright orange vinyl shoes with a buckle strap. We weren't allowed to wear them until the big day of going to the train depot, but we were as excited as kids at Christmas, and we couldn't wait - we snuck them out of the box and wore them in the bedroom.

When that day came, my sisters and I were anxious about riding the train alone. The conductor told me to listen closely, because if we missed our stop in Spokane we would continue on to Chicago. I fought to stay awake the whole way. When they called out "Spokane", my sister Cart wouldn't wake up and the train started moving again. I screamed for help, and we were finally able to get off the train. There was our mom on the platform, standing beside a new boyfriend.

Mom was living with a friend who took care of us while mom was at work. The lady did not like us at all, and she started locking us in the pantry closet during the day. On one of those days we were so hungry that we ate a package of butterscotch chips. This made her so mad that when she locked us in the next day, she took out the light bulb so we were in the dark. Sometimes we just sat in there and cried. Other times we tried to find ways to get out. When that failed we either slept or played make-believe. Our mom took us to the circus once that summer, but as soon as it was over she left with her boyfriend, and back we went to the closet.

Mom told us that Dad was coming to get us soon, to take us back home. We couldn't wait for him to get there and rescue us from the wicked lady. But later, I overheard her on the phone telling Dad she had changed her mind. I ran to pick up the other phone and yelled as loud as I could for him to come save us, telling him what was happening.

I knew going back home meant going back to the men, but I knew how to live in that. Being trapped in a closet was too much for me. I hated how the dark, closed-in place swallowed me up. Soon my dad, brother, uncle and cousin came to get us. We were going home.

After we had returned home, my aunt and uncle took me for a drive with them and my cousins one day. We stopped at Plum Point on the Columbia River. My uncle was standing out there gazing at the river, and I walked up beside him. I don't remember exactly what he said, but he was sad. He told me something about missing the good things in life while we are looking for something better. Then, he told me that he loved me. That was a very special day for me.

Soon after that was my tenth birthday. My aunt made all the preparations for my party. She and my uncle gave me a Dalmatian autograph dog, and everyone at the party signed it for me. I was happy that everyone had so much fun.

After the party, Dad, my uncle, my brother and cousin all went out together. They had too much to drink that night, and on their way home they crashed. My great grandma came to get us kids, and we found out that my uncle had been killed. The next morning a car pulled up with my Dad in the front passenger seat. He wouldn't even look at us. He just stared straight ahead saying over and over again, "I killed my brother".

I sobbed at the funeral, and I didn't stop crying for weeks. No one understood - he had told me he loved me, and now he was gone. Mom had moved back home, but nothing was good. One night when I was with Dad, I was crying again. Dad looked at me and said, "Please, Jay, you've got to stop. We all miss him, but you have to stop. It's killing me." So I stopped. I stopped feeling almost everything. It was my job to please him, and to take care of others.

My aunt told my parents she needed my help because she was hurting so badly, so I started staying nights with her. She had me sleep with her, and I listened to her cry herself to sleep. There were pills by the bed that she took every night. I knew the pills helped her feel better. They helped me, too. I needed to take care of her. It was my job.

After a while she moved away, and I was back at home enduring whatever the man who came down those stairs wanted from me. So many men - I began to hate them. I hated the voices now too. They were not my friends anymore. There were too many of them. Sometimes I didn't even know if I was real, I just did what I was told.

CHAPTER 4

In sixth through eighth grades, I spent the summers on a wheat farm, cooking meals and helping to care for their children. I didn't make much money, but I was given room and board. And every morning as the sun rose, I went out and saddled up a horse to ride, and again every evening after I finished the last of my chores.

I forgot about everything painful in my life while I was on that horse. In my mind I could still make believe the same wonderful things. I was loved, beautiful, and clean. I had parents who cared for and protected me. I had no worries in life... until I slid off that horse to put him away. That's when I thought about what the evening would bring. But I reminded myself that tomorrow was a new day, and I would ride as the sun came up. Then it was back to reality as one of the men there took me to his room.

In junior high I started talking to a boy at school who was different than others I'd met. He treated me nicely, and with respect, which was something I didn't even understand. But I liked it. Something about the way he treated me made me feel like I was a person and that I mattered. Our friendship soon developed into something more.

When I was 13 years old, something occurred that was even worse than the years of rapes. While I was on the phone with my boyfriend, I was sodomized by a man I babysat for. We'd done other sexual things before, but this time he was very angry with me. The pain was extreme and it took my breath away - I hung up the phone right away. He just smiled and said, "How do you like that?" Everything he did to me that night was sicker and dirtier than before. And I felt even dirtier than before, which was hard to imagine. A severe spiraling down was happening inside of me. I no longer had a desire to survive. I knew there must be something better after you stop living... even if it was nothing.

I became continually more hardened after this. Drug and alcohol use became a way of life. Inside I was always crying out for something more, but I didn't know what the more was. I searched fervently for places to go – I found ads for boarding schools in Arizona, New Mexico, anything I could find, especially if it involved horses. My mom repeatedly told me no, but I kept searching.

During a football game at the junior high school one night, I took every kind of pill I could get from people. I don't even know what they were - they were just a rainbow of colors in my hand. Then I went into the downstairs bathroom at the school and set a fire, hoping to just disappear. But it didn't work. Someone decided to save me. They pointed out to me that I couldn't have burned the building down - it was concrete. I was even a failure at trying to kill myself.

By the summer I was 14, my life was only getting worse. I was consumed with thoughts of ending my life. My mom and I had one of our worst arguments ever just before she left to go out with my aunt and uncle. Then a girl called to tell me my boyfriend was breaking up with me. Something broke inside. I didn't care anymore. So when a man who had been pursuing me called, I agreed to meet him. I went off with him and a group of other guys for the weekend to a cabin where there was a big party.

My parents didn't know where I was, and so police from three counties were out looking for me. When the guys took me home they didn't even bring the car to a complete stop for me to jump out. My dad was sitting out front, and the anger I expected to see wasn't there, but rather a combination of fear and relief. My mom had some angry words to say, and then the police came to take me to Juvenile Detention.

Sitting in the back of the police car, my whole insides were screaming out for help. *Is there anyone in this world who can help me understand why my life is this way? Where can I go? How can I make it all just stop?* The officer pulled over along the side of the road to have a "heart to heart" talk with me about my behavior. Then he opened the door, and my dad pulled up behind the car to get me. I was thankful that I wasn't going to jail, but was anything going to change?

In 1974 I was fifteen, and it was the year of the Expo World's Fair in Spokane. During that year, a huge growth appeared sticking out from my left ribs.

It grew quickly, and continued to get larger. X-rays revealed that it was a tumor growing between two ribs. Toward the end of the school year I had surgery, and in order to get the tumor completely out they had to remove the ends of the two ribs.

The tumor was benign, but I faced the task of learning how to sit up and walk all over again. I was missing out, and I wanted to make up for lost time after being in the hospital. I bounced back pretty quickly, got a job at a local restaurant and made great money that summer. I was determined to start enjoying life.

I had a good friend, Carmen, who encouraged me to take a huge new step in my life, and I signed up for girls' basketball and the powder puff football team. Carmen had a way of helping me see things in a positive way without telling me, "You're screwed up Jay". I was beginning to experience life in a completely different way, and enjoying it!

Then one morning on our way to school (she even came and picked me up for school) I lit up my cigarette and felt like I was going to barf all over the place. I actually had my head hanging out the window most of the way to school. When I finally went to see the doctor, he did tests and told me, "You're pregnant." As a teenager, those weren't the happiest words to hear. All of a sudden everything was changing in my life. My parents tried to get an abortion set up, and everyone had an opinion of what I should do and how I should do it. The right decision seemed obvious to everyone...except for me – it was far from simple.

On the one hand, I was finally starting to interact with others, enjoy life, be a part of school activities and just have fun. On the other hand, there was a baby inside of me who needed someone to love them, protect them, and want them. I went to my ex-boyfriend and told him the news. He wanted to keep the baby, and so did I. Not long after my 16th birthday I moved in with my boyfriend on the reservation, and I was sure life was going to be better now.

My parents filed for divorce not long after I moved out. So much division was happening. Nothing would ever be the same again.

I was sitting one day with my boyfriend's mom doing beadwork when she looked at me and asked, "Babe, who's your dad?" I told her my stepdad's name and she said, "No, who's your real dad?" I told her his name had been Gary DePue. Then she told me that she had known my dad, and had even dated him for awhile. She told me that I looked a lot like him, which was why she had thought to ask me. This information drew me even closer to her. I somehow felt like I finally belonged somewhere. She had been good to me from the beginning, had actually wanted me around. In my mind and heart she was becoming my "mom".

I worked hard to avoid drinking, getting high and smoking – I wanted to protect the baby inside me. The birth of my son, JR, was honestly the first beautiful experience I'd ever had in my life. I couldn't believe that this perfect little child had been created inside of me. It was a miracle. I felt an amazing love for him.

As much as I had always wanted my mom to love me, I realized now that I was filled with hatred for her. Now that I was a mother myself, I didn't understand how she could have allowed so much pain in her child's life.

Soon, everything began to change for the worse. Drugs became a big part of our lifestyle, and my boyfriend grew to be very violent and controlling. I was mostly kept locked away, not allowed contact with any friends or family. I was isolated again, but this time I had my beautiful son with me.

Once the beatings started, they continually got worse. When my boyfriend came home one night I was wearing a nightgown that was given to me when I'd had the baby, but I had shortened it from ankle length to just above the knees. That set him off, and within moments after coming through the door he was kicking my face in with his cowboy boots. I honestly thought that I was going to die.

The next thing I knew someone was putting me in a truck, and my boyfriend's uncle was telling me it would be okay. He tried to comfort me all the way to the hospital, but it was futile. My eyes were so badly damaged they were swollen shut. I couldn't see anything. The pain was relentless, and the questions repeating in my mind were, *"Why am I alive? Why am I here? What did I do wrong?"*

In the emergency room the doctor asked me what happened, but then I felt my boyfriend's hand and I knew I couldn't tell the truth. I told the doctor I fell off the chair while changing a light bulb. I knew it was stupid, but I was afraid and I didn't have time to calculate an intelligent lie.

I left my boyfriend after that, and tried to go back to school. But no one there would talk to me. Once again I was the freak. One day as I was starting to walk down the hall, I saw the looks – people standing at their lockers staring. Their whispers seemed so loud. Inside I felt like Alice in Wonderland, shrinking with each step, each look, each whisper. But then a friend named Casey came alongside me and walked down that hall with me to my locker. It seemed like the longest hallway in the world that day, but his act of kindness meant so much to me. I didn't understand why he would choose to walk with me, or how he could be a friend to something that looked like me. He probably didn't think twice about it, but he made me feel like someone who mattered. But with the exception of Casey's friendship, I felt like an outsider. I realized who and what I was, so I quit school and went back to my boyfriend.

During yet another visit to the emergency room, a doctor looked me in the eye and said, "The next time he hits you may be the end of your life." I wondered if there was a guarantee on that, because in my heart I wanted it. I wanted someone to put me out of my misery. But wait, what about my son? I loved him so much - what would happen to him?

After that I left town for several months. I was getting ready for a date one night when my ex-boyfriend showed up at the door. I ended up driving him back home to the reservation, and I told him it was over. He stood up and slammed his fist into the mirror, breaking it. No one ever understood how hard that was for me to do, and how much it hurt me inside to leave him. That mirror shattering was a picture of my heart.

Even though I am not a Native American, the reservation was the only place where I'd felt I fit in, the only place I'd ever been accepted. I had a deep love and respect for these people; I never once felt rejected, condemned, made fun of or sexually abused by them. So by leaving my boyfriend, I was also leaving a way of life and a family that I loved very much. I was giving up everything I had spent my childhood hoping for and dreaming of: to be a part of a family, to belong, to be wanted and loved. With that decision to leave, I began to slowly die. My shattered heart was becoming so calloused that nothing could penetrate it.

CHAPTER 5

My drug use grew to be out of control, and soon I was eating acid every other day. Why couldn't I die? I was sure I was putting enough drugs in my body to kill myself.

Then on May 30, 1976, my son was taken away from me. His dad didn't like being away from his son, and he felt that JR was not safe with me. So he took off with him to live in the mountains for awhile, and no one would tell me where he was. I missed him terribly, but I turned my focus to meeting my drug and alcohol needs.

My friend Shelley convinced me that finishing school was the best thing I could do for myself, and so I went back to school in a neighboring town with hopes of graduating. I lived with her parents at the start. Her mother, Kathleen, was a wonderful woman - small, but so strong. She was good to me. Although she was quiet, her presence was different than other women I'd been around, as if she had an authority that demanded respect. I wanted to be like her.

I came home from school one day to find my mom there, along with a new stepdad, Gene. Gene had threatened the family I was staying with, forcing them to convince me to leave with my mom. It was terribly hard to leave that day. I knew things were only going to get worse.

In the fall of 1976 I had my first mental breakdown. I was lost in a dark, dreadful prison inside of my head, and I wasn't sure I would ever get out. At the hospital I was taken to a room where there was only a bed and a very heavy door - that door frightened me, as if it was confirming that there was no escape. A counselor asked me about many different things in my life, and for the first time I told someone things I had never spoken about before. He left the room stating that there wasn't really any hope for me, and told the nurse to give me the meds I needed to just exist. *"No hope, such ugly words - no hope,"* my heart cried, but I wouldn't let them know.

By Halloween I heard from my son's father, and at last I was able to see my son. He had grown so much in the few months we'd been apart, and he was still so beautiful. JR was back with me now, but he began to go back and forth between his dad and me.

A couple months later I was rushed to the hospital with extreme pain in my abdomen. The doctor in the emergency room was more concerned with repairing all of my body scars than with what was currently wrong with me. *These scars are nothing compared to the scars inside of me*, I thought. *They go too deep to ever be fixed.* They did an emergency appendectomy, only to discover that there was nothing wrong with my appendix. I was pregnant again.

The doctor who had delivered my son, and had treated me numerous times, came to talk to me

33

about my life. He genuinely cared about me, and he believed the best thing for me to do was to have an abortion. My dad and his new wife drove me to Spokane for my first abortion in December 1976. They helped me to get a place of my own before the trip, so I could go home to it afterwards.

Soon after the abortion, I began bleeding heavily late one night and felt very weak. My little boy, not even two years old yet, was trying to help his mommy. I made it almost to the office of the motel next door, and then JR ran to the door and kept pushing the bell button until someone came out. I was hemorrhaging, and they called for an ambulance right away. That little boy saved my life.

I continued going downhill emotionally, and the more I went down, the more my drug and alcohol use went up. But inside I still wanted something different. I wanted to be a good person, to be a good mother, to have a family. I lay on my bed one night all curled up and screaming out for help. *Isn't there any other way to live? Is it only real in the movies?* I had a new deep pain now too - the abortion haunted me. How was it possible to keep dying inside, but my body kept surviving?

A family who lived on a farm outside of town took me in for the remainder of the school year. I had never been around a family anything like them before. This husband seemed to really love his wife. He never touched his daughters or me the way other men did. I was drawn to him, not in a sick way, but in curiosity.

He was sitting in the living room one day, listening to a Don Williams album. I came in and sat down on the couch, and he told me to just close my eyes and listen to the music. Inside of me I was preparing for the "Mr. Good Guy" image to be shattered, but I did as he said. With my eyes closed I began to really hear the music, and it calmed me. I can't remember the words he said to me, but I remember how good they made me feel, how kind he was, and how he didn't say or do anything sexual. It was clean, pure and kind. I knew in my heart this was a good man, but I wondered whether there were more in the world.

At last I was completing high school. Just before my graduation, I found out the name and phone number of my biological grandmother, my biological dad's mother. I called her to tell her I was graduating, and asked her to come. She started to stutter, and then a man came on the phone and told me never to call again.

I wasn't a star student, but I did graduate. I even discovered a love for plants while doing botany for my biology class project. Several teachers at the school invested time into my life, and with their help I earned my diploma.

After graduation I moved to Spokane to go to business school, where one of my great aunts was an instructor. After many weeks of school she told me that I would never succeed, that I just didn't have what it takes to be a good secretary. Regardless of how badly I wanted to finish, I believed her and walked away from it.

I looked for work, but drugs and alcohol were all that really mattered to me. What was left inside of me was dead now. I became violent and abusive, especially to my beautiful little boy. Something inside me had died after the abortion, and I never got it back.

But less than a year after the first abortion, I was going in for another. The experience was horrifying. It wasn't working. I heard awful noises and then there was panic. What I saw afterwards sent me reeling. They had lied to me. It was a baby, not a blood clot. What had I done?

I got through each day by using masks, and I had many to choose from. I had learned to become whatever I needed to be to adapt to my surroundings - cowgirl, biker, stripper, fighter, lover, prostitute – and the list just went on. I did what I had to do, and I became whatever each man wanted me to be.

I had just gotten out of jail when my son became very sick. He had spinal meningitis, and it was possible that he could die. The hospital told me I could stay in his room at night, but it was so clean in there I couldn't do it. One of my aunts offered me a place to stay at her home, but I couldn't do that either. I just didn't belong with the good. No one understood the darkness I lived in or the things I did to myself and others.

As I was sleeping out under a tree by the river with my sister and boyfriend, I began to wonder if my son was scared in that hospital. I remembered the nights I spent in the hospital as a child. I was remembering a lot of things; I had to stop. Looking at the people around me, I realized I didn't belong there. I started to hope that maybe I could turn my life into something good. I was desperate to change, but I didn't have a clue how to do it.

After JR recovered, I decided to go to the island my mom was living on, hoping that it could be a new beginning. I would like to say I tried, but I wasn't willing to give up the old lifestyle. I was always willing to relocate to someplace new, but I didn't apply any changes to my life. I expected it to be changed for me. I moved to a new level of abusing; now I was abusing the men, seducing them - a form of raping them. Hurting them, especially the kind and innocent ones, was giving me a new form of pleasure. It was definitely sick - being the best in every form, with whatever sex, bringing them to a certain point – it was now a controlling high for me, like being on a hunt for the next conquest. At the same time I knew in the back of my mind that I had to be stopped. I soon left the island and relocated back home, where my son was back and forth between his dad and me.

I was partying at a friend's house when I met Spike that winter. Everyone thought I knew him, so they had invited me over to see him while he was in town visiting from Wyoming. As we sat around getting high, all I could see was his back side. I liked what I saw, and said so. I was then introduced to "Spike" Mike English. He asked me out, but he was on the phone with a girlfriend in Wyoming when he asked me - so my answer was no.

By spring I decided to make a move. I found an apartment for rent in Waco, Texas, and I was sure I could get work there. So I saved up enough money to go. But first I went to Tacoma to say goodbye to my mom, brother and sisters. When I arrived, I found out my sister Jo was pregnant and due any day, but she didn't have a single thing for the baby. That bothered me. I got drunk in hopes that it would drown out my conscience, but it didn't work. So I had a baby shower for my sister, and I bought her most of what she needed. That was the end of my Texas dream.

CHAPTER 6

When I returned home, I was hired for a clerical position with a construction company. I loved this job and the people I worked with. While I was at work I was almost a different person. I thrived in an office atmosphere. I learned new clerical skills, and I was doing payroll and other bookkeeping. As much as I enjoyed it, when I left that office at the end of my shift reality was waiting for me. *You are not on this earth to enjoy life; you're here for men's pleasure. That's it.*

In June as I was on my way to a party with a friend, I ran into Spike. He followed us to the party and then spent that night with me. After that he continued to stay at my apartment.

Spike never had any money. He bummed cigarettes and everything else off my roommate and me. When I got home after working all day, most of my beer would be gone. He did keep the apartment incredibly clean, but finally I couldn't handle it any longer. I told him to leave and not come around until he had a job. I couldn't believe how many people felt sorry for him. My friends accused me of being mean for pushing him to get a job.

Spike did go to work, briefly, and we got back together. But I was on a downward spiral that was gaining speed. During a party at my house one night, my sister Jo convinced me to ride with her to show a couple of cowboys the way to a local bar. In my gut I knew it was a bad idea, but I agreed, thinking it would take only a few minutes.

The cowboys were headed out of town to a stampede, and proceeded to take us with them. They refused to let me out of the car, and my sister was upset that I was protesting so much. I'd already had way too much to drink, and by the time we got there I was an emotional mess. What happened next was nothing unusual, the rape and beating. It was a bad one too, messed up my ribs and face pretty good. An old friend, Casey, saw it happen and actually wanted to help me, but the big guy would have killed him. All I could do was scream, *"Noooo!"*

Not much later, I lost my job because of drinking and using. My boss insisted I had such talent in the work field, and he considered me an excellent employee, when I was there. But the using had gotten so bad I couldn't get out of bed most days.

I went to the post office to get my mail one day, and there was a big fat envelope. I opened it to find hundreds of dollars in cash with a note that said "Make your trip to Texas". I'm not sure why, but I had dreamed of going to Texas. Larry, a man I had been dating, believed it would help me so he sent the money. He took very good care of me and treated me like I was something special, but I didn't know how to respond to that kind of treatment. Larry was a nice guy who didn't deserve to be tied up with garbage like me.

Soon I was on my way to Texas on a greyhound bus, free at last. It was a hot day, so as we were driving between Spokane and Coeur d'Alene I went to the bathroom to change my clothes. When I came out, everyone was looking out the side window asking, "Who's Jaylene?" I looked out the window to see a car driving alongside the bus with Spike in the passenger seat, and a big sign saying "Come back, Jaylene, I love you". I didn't understand why he couldn't just let me go. Nothing was going to stop me from going to Texas this time.

But as it turned out, life in Texas was no better than my life had been anyplace else. What I experienced there was definitely not good. I don't know why I had expected it to be any different.

After less than a month I returned to Washington, and I decided to marry Spike. I had always been against marriage, but I'd tried everything else, so, I thought, why not this?

A couple weeks before the wedding, I ended up back in one of my favorite places on the reservation with a guy I knew there. We spent the night at a bartender's place, and I got to talking to her the next morning. When I told her I didn't have the money for a real wedding dress, she said she would loan me hers. She was divorced now and she thought maybe it would bring better luck to me.

Before the wedding day I told Spike that I could never be faithful to him. In my mind, I believed that this was the greatest gift I could give him, that it was what every man wanted. I was wrong. It was obviously not what he wanted to hear, and I couldn't figure out why.

The day of our wedding was hysterical. My sister Jo, who was pregnant again, was in the back room puking. She was supposed to be the maid of honor. Spike, his best man, and one of the groomsmen were out in front of the church getting high. And I was still drunk from my party the night before. As I was walking down the aisle, my dad said, "You don't have to go through with this. We can turn around right now, run out the door, head to the next town and just get drunk."

I also heard comments from the sidelines: "Give it six months"; "Won't last a week"; "She's so mean she'll probably kill him within a week!" Didn't anyone believe there was anything good in me? But I was a fighter, and all that did was push me to go through with it.

Spike thought he could save me. He didn't realize the truth about the life I lived. He didn't know about my extreme addiction to pornography, along with all of the other sexual addictions. But he was about to experience it all. He had lived pretty much a "Beaver Cleaver" life before me. Now he was entering a nightmare from hell.

The morning after our wedding, Spike left for the Tri-Cities to work. I stayed with his parents while he was gone, which was awkward to say the least. I tried extra hard to behave myself and to be faithful, since it apparently bothered Spike to think of me being with someone else. Soon I made a trip to spend some time with him in the Tri-Cities.

One morning I got up to fix him breakfast before he went to work. I was so excited about doing this. I felt like I was being the "good wife", just like in the happy family movies I'd seen. I was filled with more delight than I know how to describe. Then Spike walked into the kitchen and said, "I don't eat breakfast - gotta go." I was crushed. I took it all wrong. We never talked with each other about it, so it came between us. All the other guys who lived in the house loved that breakfast.

It wasn't long before Spike lost his job, and we moved to Medical Lake. This was our first place together alone. My son JR was with us, too. I still liked to escape to make-believe land in my mind, where I could dream that my life was good. Most days I lived in make believe more than in reality.

CHAPTER 7

We soon discovered that I was pregnant with child number two, which was a miracle considering I had an IUD in place when I conceived. The doctor said I would miscarry when they removed it, but apparently the baby thought differently.

Spike needed to find work but he wasn't having any luck. He made a trip back to Wyoming to try, but he came back unsuccessful. So one night I said, "Give me the number of your old boss." I called and introduced myself as Spike's wife. The man on the phone laughed. That made me mad, but I continued to approach him with an offer for hiring my husband. At the end of the conversation, the man got serious and said, "I've got to see this. You tell him to be here the first of April."

We moved to Wyoming in an old 1946 Ford truck that had no heater or defroster, and only one windshield wiper. Everything we owned, which wasn't much, was loaded in the back and covered with a canopy. We bundled ourselves with piles of blankets, and mounted a little fan on the dash to use as a defroster. We looked like we came out of the hills, a modern-day heading west adventure. An adventure it definitely was; we created some fantastic memories. We sang so many rounds of Old MacDonald Had a Farm that to this day I dislike that song.

In September of 1980 I gave birth to Andy, our 8-pound baby boy. He'd gone a few weeks overdue and the delivery was rough, but he was worth it all. At night when I was up nursing him, I wanted to be able to sing to him, but I didn't know the words to any nice, peaceful songs except one - Silent Night. So that's what I sang to him every night for months. I'm not sure if it was the peacefulness of the song or sheer boredom that put him to sleep.

Spike was making very good money, but we could barely afford to live because of my drug and alcohol habit. Things became increasingly more strained between us. Spike's way of building himself up in the eyes of others was by downgrading me. He made cruel jokes about me, and when that didn't work he exposed my flaws in front of his friends and family. Soon I was spending most of my time with some local bikers in town, and less time with my husband. I usually brought the children along with me. My mentality was that at least they were with me, even if it was while I was getting high.

I was trained to never tell a man no to anything sexual, so unfortunately adultery was another destructive force in our marriage. Sadly, I was also an exhibitionist. So it didn't matter where we were or how many people were around, I would strip and be sexually active in front of everyone. This sexual addiction increased as strongly as the drug cravings. Nothing mattered - man, woman, two, three or more people at a time.

I worked hard to keep this part of my life secret. I told Spike the truth about certain sexual acts with men at the bars, but only enough to ease his suspicions. I couldn't get enough. The pornography was a powerful tool for seducing women. And I sought out virgin men to ensnare, as if I was driven to take something from them that had been taken from me. I got a high from seeing the pain I caused in people's lives. The very things I hated as a child I now lived by my own choice. I was no longer the victim - I was the predator, no better than any man who ever violated me.

I began to disappear for days at a time. I started drinking in one place and ended up hundreds of miles away. Then I came to in a panic not knowing where I was, and sometimes who I was with. I'd find a pay phone to call Spike, and he would talk me down to a calm place so he could figure out where I was. When I got home I cleaned up for a few days, tried to be good, and then I'd snap all over again.

Spike and I wanted to try to change our lives, so we went to a church with Spike's brother and sister-in-law. They didn't believe in using musical instruments in that church, and I'm not sure what else. We were baptized in the dead of winter, and the water in that baptismal was icy cold. We didn't bring a change of clothes, so we walked out into the cold night air soaking wet. We were trying to do our part to become good.

I was a big fan of wrestling, and several of my biker friends were over one day to watch it with us and have a few beers. While they were there, some women from the church came by. Those women proceeded to order my friends out of my house - that was the end of being good for me! I told them to get out and never come back. No one could tell me what kind of friends to have, what to watch, or what I should or shouldn't drink. My dislike for Christians grew stronger at that point.

My violence was another detriment to our marriage. I physically beat on Spike, chased him with knives, and actually begged him to beat me. It was hard for me to believe that he loved me because he was so kind to me. That did not compute in my head. All I had ever known and experienced in love was connected to some form of pain: physically, emotionally, or sexually. In my mind, by abusing him I was proving my love.

On one occasion we were sitting in a bar in Wyoming with my mother and stepfather when I started describing how I was going to slit Spike's throat. My mom was so terrified she became hysterical. That night I ended up in a violent rage so extreme that my stepfather (a golden gloves boxer over 6 feet tall and well over 200 pounds, who had spent most of his life in prison) was afraid to enter the house to help Spike. He believed that what raged in me was not natural. He was right, but I didn't understand it.

I honestly wanted to be different, to get my life straightened out, but how? My mom had been going to an Assemblies of God church, so I decided to give church a try once again. The tumor that had been removed from my left ribs during my sophomore year had reoccurred, and the night before I was to have surgery to remove it I went to a Sunday evening service at the church. When they learned about my tumor, the people laid their hands on me and prayed for me to be healed. I thought they were wacky, but I behaved myself until they were done.

The next morning I checked into the hospital, and they took x-rays to get updated pictures before the surgery. Afterwards, the doctor marched into my room yelling, asking me what I had done between Friday and this morning. I didn't understand what he wanted to know. I hadn't done anything wrong. I told him exactly what I had done, including the weird church thing the previous night.

He said, "A tumor that size does not just go away!" He fell back in the chair and put his head in his hands. He kept insisting that it couldn't be gone. He had multiple x-rays of it, and it couldn't just disappear! He decided he was going to open me up anyway. I didn't understand any of it. Was the tumor really gone? How could it be? Did that prayer stuff really work? Was God real? And if He was real, did this mean maybe He liked me?

The biopsy showed no signs of cancer. The doctor built a set of mesh ribs to replace the ones that had been missing for years. After surgery the scrub nurse came into my room. She sat at the edge of the bed and thanked me. She was a born again believer but had walked away from God because of things that occurred in her life. But witnessing what she did that morning reminded her of how great our God is. She had recommitted her life to Him. I didn't understand a single thing that was going on with the doctor, the nurse, my body or God! I hadn't done anything; I didn't even believe!

Shortly after this I moved into an apartment of my own. This was the second time Spike and I had separated. My sexual relationships with women were taking over the desire to be with men, and I knew how my husband felt about homosexuality. I focused on keeping this hidden.

After some time we reconciled again; but by 1984 there'd been more than enough damage done. I continued to pull Spike more and more into the depths of the perversions I lived in daily. He was entering my prison of darkness without even realizing what was happening. I didn't think it was possible to ever save our marriage, so I moved back to Washington. But I was gone only a week when we talked on the phone, and decided that I would fly back and then drive home with him. I think we were addicted to the sickness of one another's lifestyles as much as to any drug. We were no good together, yet miserable apart.

Within a few months of returning to Washington, Spike enlisted in the Army.

CHAPTER 8

While Spike was in basic training I lived with his folks. During this time I pushed myself to change. I tried to quit the drugs, unsuccessfully, so I quit some of them. I did cut back on the drinking, and I was being faithful to him while he was gone. To me this was an enormous accomplishment, because I'd never been able to do that before.

I tried to be everything I'd seen in those family TV shows, but it was never quite right. I was trying to be somebody else. But if that wasn't me, then what was? I had mastered the art of being a chameleon throughout my life, able to change appearance to blend in everywhere I went. It didn't matter what kind of lifestyle it was - rodeo, biker, native, junky, even prim and proper - I adapted and became what was needed to survive. Who was the real Jaylene?

When Spike finished basic training we moved to Fort Polk, Louisiana. Within two weeks I was pregnant. But during this pregnancy, I couldn't seem to quit using or drinking. My body kept trying to miscarry, and the doctors kept giving me injections to stop the aborting process. After I was into the fifth month they said they could no longer do anything to save the baby. I tried to stop, as much as was naturally possible, but the best I could do was to cut back on the drugs by increasing the alcohol.

During the eighth month the baby had not moved for over a week, and I felt sick. The doctor was unable to find a heartbeat, and he told me the baby had died. They said they needed to deliver the baby to remove it before I got any worse. I lost all control and just ran.

I went home, got into the bath tub and I prayed. "If there really is a God out there somewhere, then please, please, don't take this baby girl. I know it's my fault, but don't let her die like this. If you are real, I will turn my life around and do whatever it is you want me to." Within moments that baby was moving all over the place, and I was terrified! I was overjoyed, but afraid at the same time because of what I had just witnessed. This was real! Now what?

In January 1986, I gave birth to a beautiful baby girl, Carly. It was undeniably a miracle she was alive. The placenta was far from being any shade of pink. It was grayish-black and it disintegrated each time the doctor touched it. The doctor explained to my husband what that meant, and seeing those two people look at me with such anger and disgust was more than I could handle. The fighter in me emerged, and I turned away from them as if I were the person being wronged.

The following day I was taken into the operating room where they tied my tubes. I did not deserve to have children - that's what everyone agreed. *What is wrong with me? Why can't I be good? Why can't I just stop?* I had done treatment,

I'd worked the programs, I'd done everything I knew to do to stop and I just couldn't. Everyone insisted that AA had such high success rates - just not for me. I didn't know where else to turn for help.

Spike was reassigned to a new duty station in Baumholder, West Germany. During the process of obtaining our passports, they were unable to find any record of my birth. My birth certificate had been altered when I was just a few months old. The last name had been changed legally, and the information for my father had been changed from unknown. It now listed one of my step-grandfathers as the father. My passport approval was on hold because of questionable identity. *Questionable identity?* How ironic! I was questioning my identity myself, *"Who are you Jaylene?"*

In the meantime, our neighbors had been inviting us to come to church with them. We were dragging our feet on this issue. We had tried it before and God just didn't work for us. But after one particularly bad day, we agreed to go and try again.

As it turned out, a traveling evangelist was speaking who had not been scheduled. It was a last minute event. She gave an altar call, and I had a strange feeling that I needed to go forward, so I did. She was moving along, praying over each person. However, when she came to me she fell back to the floor very dramatically. She was shouting something about the love of God on me being so powerful. I thought to myself, "That's it; she's a fake - because everyone knows that God cannot and does not love someone like me." I left that church hurting even more, because I wanted so desperately to believe what she had spoken about me, but I couldn't.

Finally, all of the passports were completed and we were preparing to leave for Germany - except for my oldest son JR. He did not want to go with us. This was hard for me, but he returned to Washington to live with my mother.

Germany was absolutely beautiful. I loved everything about it. I earnestly wanted to be a new person there, to make a new start at life. No one there knew anything about my past, and I knew I could be a good person. It seemed I had always been searching for a new life. Maybe this was my chance.

But soon I had a rude awakening from my dream of living a good life. I decided to go onto the post where Spike was stationed to see him during his lunch break. I put on a dress and tried to look "good" for him. But when I entered the building, I received far too much attention from the other men, and the tension started. He was angry and I didn't know why. I was being good, but good was never enough.

Eventually I got involved with another man from his unit, and not secretly either. I did whatever I wanted right in front of him and everyone else. It was killing Spike, but it was killing me too. All I had wanted was to be his wife. The old Jaylene was back worse than she'd ever been. I was done making-believe and wishing for a good, clean life. Hatred and anger were rising from deep within me like never before.

A woman named Bonnie from Mississippi was living in the flat above us. Bonnie was a Christian, but she treated me like any other person. She actually started drawing me into some "good" things in life, like going for walks to the creek in the village to feed the ducks. I never imagined that I would enjoy sitting and feeding ducks, but I liked it. She told me a lot of things about Jesus, and I in return shared things with her about life from my perspective.

I was especially high one day when Bonnie came downstairs. She broke down into tears, telling me how much it hurt her to see me like this. I cussed and told her if she didn't want to see me like this she should get out of my house. It was that easy for me – or at least it used to be. Something was happening in my heart. Hurting people was beginning to hurt me too. I didn't understand it.

I tried to be a "good girl" in the daylight, but I was sick and perverted at night. Too sloppy with everything, I couldn't keep things hidden any more. One of the men stationed nearby found out about his wife and me. He had been passed out on the couch while I had his wife in my bedroom introducing her to things she could never have imagined. He was disgusted, and she was crushed - she never would have gone to those places of perversion if she had been sober... most people wouldn't. I felt bad for her, but didn't she understand that this was life?

Then one day I went too far. I would be going home to the states. Until then I had thought I wanted to leave, but now I didn't. I wanted out of my old lifestyle, but I couldn't bring myself to tell Spike, Bonnie, or anyone in authority that I was wrong. I no longer wanted to be a "Harley honey", as the German bikers called me. I truly wanted to be Spike's honey, to be Mrs. English. I wanted a life that was not available to someone like me, and it was killing me inside.

On December 12, 1986, I boarded a plane to the U.S., leaving Spike behind. As the plane was nearing Newfoundland, fire erupted in the cargo hold. We were told to prepare for an emergency landing evacuation. A woman near me screamed, "Oh my God, we're going to crash into the ocean!" We weren't over land. I was alone with my 11-month-old daughter and 6-year-old son, and it was my choices that were bringing them to this kind of death. In desperation, I began crying out to God.

A man came up from behind and sat next to me. "Don't worry," he said, "I'll help the boy and you take care of the baby." Everything happened fast after that. The plane made it to dry land, but the landing was hard and painful. I could not see my son anywhere in the chaos. An attendant told me to slide down the emergency ramp. Once on land, I still could not find him. We were transported by emergency vehicles to a building on the military base.

The man in charge was frantic, shouting things fast. I asked someone nearby what was wrong with him. They told me that a year ago to the day a military plane had crashed here with no survivors, killing over 250 soldiers. This man had worked that emergency also.

Once we got to the evacuation building I found my son. But then when I looked down my daughter was gone. Andy and I searched all over and finally found Carly with her arms wrapped around the leg of a biker. He must have seen the panicked look on my face because he called to me and asked, "Does this belong to you?" Thank God, both children were alive and safe. Carly had a cut up lip from the impact of the landing, but otherwise she was fine. I never did find the man from the plane to tell him thank you for helping my son. We waited for hours until a plane from New York arrived and was loaded with everything from the other plane.

When I arrived back home I was able to contact Spike in Germany. I then learned that at the same time our plane was on fire, the apartment we lived in had caught on fire. Bonnie's husband was able to get in to save Spike, who was passed out. After that Spike went AWOL, and in a sense so did I. I was living out the same bad choices all over again, but on an even worse scale than before. When Spike reported back to his unit, he was given an honorable discharge and sent back to the states.

CHAPTER 9

That summer of 1987, my son JR attended a Salvation Army camp. I didn't want him going, fearful that he would reveal things about my lifestyle. But my cousin Nina persuaded me to allow him to go have fun, and Spike agreed that he should go. While he was there, JR asked them to pray that his mom would accept Jesus and quit using drugs.

By August of 1987, I had sunk lower than I had ever been before. Death was not coming - I tried persistently but it wouldn't happen. Crawling home on my hands and knees from the tavern one night, I thought maybe someone would run over me. But not a single car was on the road. Within days, I put more cocaine into my body than I ever had before. People were standing back away from me as if I was going to physically explode like dynamite.

When a man named Rick asked me to leave with him one night, I asked if I could drive his car, and he foolishly said yes. I felt badly that he would be hurt, but I had to end the torment I was living in. I put my foot to the floor, hoping to go airborne at the curve and into the river. But I wasn't able to control the steering of the car, so that attempt failed as well. At that point I literally gave up. I couldn't even succeed at suicide.

Now I had another craving - to hurt others. I fantasized about cutting people, watching the blood flow. When I looked at the water running over the dam, I was fascinated with how the water turned to blood before my eyes. I became obsessed with the idea of killing. It seemed I wanted it more than the sex and drugs now.

Each day I was living a slow, tormenting death inside. It was a deep, agonizing, emotional worthlessness. Tormenting darkness - dark, lonely, and unreachable, with no hope - that's what my life had been.

I was at home in bed when I felt myself leaving my body, as had happened many times before with overdoses. I knew that just like all the other times, something was going to save me. Not this time. I heard a voice that I cannot describe. It was strong, not loud, but strong, and it asked me one thing: "Do you know where you're going when you die?"

Of course I knew, to the biggest party of all time - hell. But then in that instant, I knew it was not going to be a party at all. It was going to be even worse than everything I'd already lived through. How could that be? How could death be worse? Yet somehow I knew with everything inside of me that it was true. I was about to enter a place of torture and torment that was beyond my imagination.

I yelled out to Spike to hang on to me, because I was leaving my body. He responded, "You're just too high again. Leave me alone." For the first time in my life I was afraid of death, not welcoming it. *Stop! I don't want to go to hell, not now, please!* It did stop, just as fast as it had started.

Everything began to unfold within a matter of days after that. The first exposure was that Spike and I discovered we were sexually involved with the same woman. Then he began to learn about all the things I had been caught up in. All of the lies were being exposed.

Things were changing too fast. My mind couldn't sort, plan, or find an escape. Make-believe wasn't working either. I was coming face to face with it all, and there was no place to run and hide. What was uglier - the things done to me, or the things I had done? I didn't know.

Within a few days, Spike walked into the kitchen and told me to pack my stuff and the kids' clothes. He was sending me with my mom to go back to Tacoma. This was it, I thought, he was really done with me. I begged him not to make me leave, but he wouldn't give in. Then my ex-brother-in-law pulled up. I yelled to him for help as I was being put in my mom's car. He looked me in the eyes and said, "Jay, you need help. You're out of control." I couldn't believe it. He was siding with Spike. Everyone was against me, and they were sending me with my mom, the person who resented my life the most.

I decided that if I had to go, I wasn't going to let anyone be happy about it. Two hours into the trip, I told my mom I needed to make a stop, so we stopped in the next town where I was able to hook up with an old ex. He spent the night getting me all the coke he could. The problem was that it was never enough. I gave him permission to do whatever he wanted to me all night, as long as he kept feeding me the coke. He made me many promises that night, and all I had to do was say yes to moving in with him. He would keep me supplied and take care of me, he said. I promised to be back. Spike had dumped me - I had to look out for myself, and this might be my last resort.

When we arrived in Tacoma, I was all used up and no good to anyone, as usual. We lived not far from a local stroll, so I figured that was my next step - head to the street that night to make some money. But what happened next stopped me in my tracks. Spike pulled up in a U-haul truck loaded with everything we owned. What was he doing there? Did he come to say good-bye, or to take the kids from me? Maybe I could barely walk, but I could still stir up a horrifying rage when I needed to fight, and that was what he was going to get.

But you could have knocked me over with a feather when I learned that he wasn't there to say good-bye, he was there to stay. He went to the apartment complex office and got us an apartment of our own. He told me he never planned to leave me. He just needed to get me out of town.

What was happening? Was he sincere or was it a set up? It was hard for me to know what to believe. My mind could not be trusted most of the time. I was risking the possibility of ending up out on my own, but I made a call to my old ex to cancel my moving plans. "I want another chance with my husband," was all I said.

CHAPTER 10

I wanted to try again to be good, but my body was fighting it, and the cravings were too much. I met a contact in the apartment above us who was willing to give me a chance at running for him. By the 27th of September, I was nearly dead physically, mentally and definitely emotionally. I looked like a holocaust victim, weighing all of about 98 pounds. I could hardly walk on my own, let alone conquer three little stairs. I had become an invalid, a prisoner of my own choices. I had done this to myself.

That morning Spike told me we were going to go to church with my mom. Not that again! This was stupid. It didn't work, so why did we keep trying? Spike would not let up, and if he got upset he might not get my next fix for me. I dressed in my favorite jeans - the butt was ripping away from the Harley wings patch, but oh well – and a sexually graphic t-shirt with no bra or underwear. I looked in the mirror and told myself I looked good. I thought, "If I'm going to church, I'm going to be real about it." So I got myself fixed up on a good enough high to hold me for at least an hour.

Church was lasting more than an hour. "Come on, let's get out of here," I kept saying. No one listened to me. The voices in my head were screaming at me to run. They were warning me about these church people and what they would do to judge and condemn me. *God doesn't care about you. If He did, then why didn't He stop all of those terrible things that happened in your life?*

I'd heard these same things over and over growing up. I knew that I was one of those who were not "chosen by God", but "used by God" as an example of how bad life could be if you leave Him. *I know, I know, shut up - everyone just shut up and leave me alone!* There was a screaming happening inside me that I didn't recognize.

Then a song started, "Just as I am…" *No, make it stop!* That's all that kept screaming inside my head. My body was sick and in terrible pain, and this song was making it worse. It felt as if it was burning my skin. It was torturous. I put my hands over my ears to block the sound. I looked at my mother and saw fear on her face, along with that familiar "You're embarrassing me" look that she got when she was in public with me. Then I looked over at Spike, and he was standing. What was he doing? Was he going down there? Then I was angry. "Fine, he can go, but not me. I don't need any of you."

Then a hand grabbed my wrist and started dragging me. *Fight, fight! You've got to fight them!* I started fighting and cussing out the most vulgar words as I was being dragged down the aisle. Wait - it was my husband doing this. What was he doing?

Next I saw a little man up front, the pastor, with wire rimmed glasses and a shocked look on his face. He kept tapping his hands together. Was he afraid? Then he changed the song. What was that they were singing now? "In the name of Jesus, in the name of Jesus, demons will have to flee." WHAT? Were they calling me a demon? Was this like one of those vampire movies where they drive a stake through your heart? What were they going to do to me?

Spike wouldn't stop and all I could see were suits, fur coats, and faces full of fear and disgust. I recognized the looks. They meant tramp, garbage, worm food - I had heard it all and seen it in people's eyes too many times before. Damn, how I hated Christians. They were weak, judging, hypocritical dogs.

When we got about three steps from the altar, Spike looked me in the eye and said, "I can't live like this any longer. Something has got to change." Was he going to leave me now, after everything we'd been through? Who would take care of me? Then he turned away and knelt at the altar. I have never felt such respect for any human being as I did when I saw Spike bowing down as he did. Why? What was it? What was he doing? What should I do now?

I knelt down at the same altar. I don't remember doing it, or even what I prayed. But I do remember looking up at a woman's face. She told me, "Your life is just beginning." And I was not dope sick at all. There was no pain in my body, no screaming voices in my head, nothing. But there was something there I had never experienced before. What was that feeling? Was it the ultimate high I'd been searching for? Then a gentle whispering voice said, *"Peace"*.

As awesome as all this was, when we got outside to the car I was already angry. I lit up a cigarette, and I was instantly sick. I had never in my life said I wanted to quit smoking, never - but now I'd been delivered from it. I fought hard to get it back, and I did, but soon after I wanted it to be gone from my life. So I willingly crushed my cigarettes at the altar of a ministry event we attended.

Each day I was increasingly more amazed at the sense of peace and purity I was experiencing. I had never felt this clean in my life. At the same time I was afraid of it going away, afraid it would just disappear like it did for Cinderella. I wanted so desperately to know who God was, to thank Him for everything He'd done.

I soon discovered that the church did not know what to do with someone like me. How should I live now? What should I do, think, say? Who was going to teach me? Would there be new men and women to show me how to please them? At once there was a voice in my head, but it wasn't loud, cruel or more than one – just one soft voice – *"You will not learn to please them, you are Mine now."* Somehow I knew at that moment that everything about how I had lived was wrong. So it made sense to do the opposite of everything I had known before.

65

CHAPTER 11

I started attending a weekly women's Bible study, and when I arrived a woman invited me to join her. Her name was Kay, and she was the leader for this small group at her table, so I would be with her each week. I couldn't help but stare - she was one of the most beautiful and elegant ladies I'd ever seen. She told me that she would be praying for me regularly, and that I would definitely become a warrior for Christ. *"Whatever that is - I am giving up fighting,"* I thought.

A few weeks later Kay spoke with me alone at the table. She opened her Bible and took out a picture to show me. I stared at the scene. It was a Native American woman on skid row. It hurt me to see it. "That was me, Jaylene," she said. I looked up in disbelief, as she nodded her head yes. She had been sober for many years now. "Could God do that for me?" I cried. "It's only been a few weeks, but if I could make it thirty days that would be awesome. Do you think I could make it a year?" Kay looked me in the eye and told me that I was going to be clean and sober for a long time and serving the Lord with my whole heart. I can't even describe the love, hope and excitement I felt when she spoke those words. Kay mentored me and encouraged me to be "me", whoever that was. It was the beginning of an interesting journey to find the real Jaylene.

A few other women began to mentor me in the area of appearance. Hole-filled jeans, crude shirts and lack of undergarments were far from modest. I'd never been taught about modesty before, so this was all new. The next thing I knew I was standing in front of my bathroom mirror crying, because I looked like a frumpy old lady. I didn't like it, but I supposed that was the way it had to be.

I was hungry to learn all that I could about God and His ways, but I had a hard time comprehending what I read or heard. The years of drugs had caused substantial damage to my brain cells. Doctors told me the damage was permanent because the cells do not regenerate. Something inside of me couldn't accept that, but I didn't know what to do or who to go to. I'd already proven to be too much for the church to know what to do with.

During a Wednesday evening church service, a woman stood up to share her testimony. She stated that she had been a "tar baby" for many years. When I heard that, my ears were miraculously opened and for the first time I was able to understand every word someone spoke. The heroin had caused so much brain damage that she couldn't read or understand what people said. So she began to pray for healing for her brain. That had been just over a year before, and now she was praising God for complete healing of her brain. My insides shouted, "Yes, I can do that, and it won't be a year for my healing!" That was in November of 1987.

During another service I looked around at the people during praise and worship; they looked so bored as they were singing. I leaned over and asked Pat, my counselor, why they weren't excited. She told me that life gets in the way. I said, "No way! I've finally got life." She told me to pray that the fire of love for God which I had inside me would be protected.

Around that same time a special speaker came to the church. She shared her story of how she was violently raped and became pregnant. God had worked a miraculous healing and restoration in her life as he empowered her to overcome the trauma she experienced. Her testimony greatly encouraged me and I wanted to thank her.

I spotted her with a group of ladies in the foyer, and she was laughing with them until I approached to speak to her. Then her facial expression quickly changed. I recognized that look. It was the one that said, "You're worthless, damaged goods." It took a lot for her to speak just a minute or two with me. It took even more from me emotionally. For some reason I thought it would be different in the church. Kay later explained to me that it really couldn't be different, because the church was made up of people. And where there are people, there are always going to be one or more who are a major work in progress.

Not long after Spike and I accepted the Lord, Spike asked us one day not to call him Spike any more. He wanted to go by Mike now. Mike and I were so excited about our new life spiritually. For the first time we had hope that life could be good.

We were on welfare at that time, but every month when we got our check we tithed 10%, and we were excited about doing it. We applied for housing assistance in December and were placed on a lengthy waiting list. But in January the Housing Authority told us that we had been moved up on the list. They showed us a house in Spanaway that was available, and it was brand new! I couldn't believe it. I'd never even been inside a new home before. Even the appliances were new, with the tags still attached. We were able to move in to that house with a rent payment of $72 per month.

We found a church that was about half an hour's walk from the house, so we started attending there. This church was smaller than the other, and we fell in love with the people. A few weeks after we moved, a couple from the first church came to see us. They had bought us a car, a little Ford Pinto wagon. Was this for real? Did people really do such things? We tried to thank them, but they insisted that it wasn't really from them, but from the Lord.

I began helping in the 4th grade Sunday school class each week, and I formed a special bond with a Down's syndrome girl named Mary. She dared me to try to memorize the scripture verse of the month. I knew I couldn't do it, but I said, "We'll see." On July 3, 1988, I stood before those children and spoke out my first memorized scripture: John 14:27, "Peace I leave with you, my peace I give to you; not as the world gives do I give to you. Let not your heart be troubled, neither let it be afraid." Mary was my biggest cheerleader, such a precious gift from God. I saw so much beauty in this creation of God's that the world labeled as defective. I've never forgotten her wonderful spirit and excitement for life.

Within just a few moments after speaking that scripture verse there was a knock on the classroom door. It was someone looking for me, so I stepped outside the room to speak with them. "Your stepfather has died, and your mom wants you to come over." I was sad at hearing the news, but not devastated. My stepfather had a severe drug habit and a lot of other issues. I had never felt comfortable around him, so we weren't very close at all. *Am I still hard hearted*, I wondered. But despite that, I couldn't get over the excitement of having memorized a verse.

By this time I felt like I was living in a fairytale world. I was fearful that something bad was going to happen and it would all disappear. Good things had never happened in my life without an extremely painful cost. Was this going to last?

CHAPTER 12

In the fall of 1988 I attended a conference that taught about the power of prayer and fasting, and afterwards I began a fast to apply the principles I learned. That night our son Andy, who was 8 years old, woke up screaming hysterically in the middle of the night. I jumped out of bed and nearly passed out because of the lack of food. Andy was burning up with a fever, so Mike loaded him into the car and took him to the hospital.

After waiting a long time to be seen, he was diagnosed with a ruptured appendix, and they said it would be a few hours before they could operate. By the time I got to the hospital it had been almost 12 hours since it had started, and they were just now preparing to take him into surgery. I spent a great deal of time in the chapel praying, even though they had told us that everything would be fine. Something inside me felt sick, like things were not right.

When the doctor came out to speak to us after surgery, he wouldn't even look us in the eye. He just stared at the floor and said he was so sorry, but our son would not live much longer. "Oh, my God, no! No! This can't be happening," I cried. "This isn't real! Please, someone tell me this isn't real." The appendix hadn't ruptured as they thought. It had literally exploded inside of his body. The poisons had been running through his system for hours, and they had no way to flush it all out. Humanly, there was no way to save him.

I went back to that chapel and prayed with all my heart. I begged God to take me instead of him. Then I went to the room where Andy was. His skin was deathly gray and clammy cold. How could my son be singing in the church kids' choir so full of life the night before, and now his life was ending? I went back and forth between his room and the chapel, each time feeling like I would collapse when I saw him.

The final time I prayed this: "Father, thank you for allowing me to be a real mother to Andy, even if it was only for a year. I love this child so much, but I understand that You love him even more. He doesn't belong to me, but to You. And now I ask that You would just protect him and relieve him from any suffering. Help me to continue to be a better mother to my other children while they are here on this earth." When I left that chapel I was full of peace. I knew I could go in and kiss my son goodbye, assured that I would see him in heaven one day.

As I got closer to his room I heard people yelling, and I knew it was over. I wondered why they were so hysterical. I looked down at my son - his skin was perfectly pink and his eyes were opening. No one could explain it. He was going to live! Everything started spinning in my head. This was a true miracle.

Andy's hospital room was full of the Holy Spirit's presence at all times. So much so that the doctors were uncomfortable when making their rounds, so they examined him, reviewed the chart, and then continued their discussions outside of the room.

As Mike and I sat in the room one night, Mike told me he was interested in another woman. She was someone he worked with, and he was lusting after her in a big way. I was stunned. So many changes had happened in a year: salvation, a new lifestyle, becoming able to truly be a mother and a wife, almost losing a child - and now this?

I had turned completely away from the sexual addictions and pornography when I accepted Christ; I just assumed he had too. But I was so on fire for God, and so focused on learning and growing in this new life that I had been neglecting Mike. What was I supposed to do now? The old Jaylene would have pulled a knife on him or ripped his face off. What was the new Jaylene supposed to do? What were the basic rules for life now? I didn't know, so I just shut down. Focus on my son, that's what I told myself

Andy was discharged and in excellent health within two days after his surgery. The doctors said it would be recorded in the medical journals. I just knew it was recorded in my heart.

Once we were home, I had to deal with the situation with Mike. I quickly learned that I couldn't confide in others. "You're too open about your past, Jaylene - some things are just too personal," they'd say. "God will take care of it." So that's exactly

73

where I went when I was hurting, upset, or confused. I ran to God. I spent time deep in worship and prayer, and I knew He was showing me what to do with each step I took. He seemed so close to me. I knew that He would always have the answer. People would say to me "I know" or "I understand what you're going through" - warning flags each time. I would just shut down. Soon I quit communicating with people in general, it seemed.

I began to pray for God to expose the situation and bring Mike to a place of repentance. Not long after that he was offered a new job working for a strong Christian man in a construction business. This provided a valuable time of training and accountability for Mike.

CHAPTER 13

By summer of 1989 we made the decision to move back to eastern Washington. My oldest son JR was very upset about this move. He really enjoyed the youth group at our church and the relationships he'd developed. We moved to Spokane in late June, and the home we rented was only a few blocks from a church.

But our experience at that church was disappointing. During worship I looked like a fanatic, because I was the only person in the church who was standing. The pastor even asked me why I did it. I earnestly prayed for direction for where we should go to church.

The pastor's wife from our church in Spanaway told us about a church in the Spokane Valley, Grace Harvest Fellowship, where her daughter was head of the children's ministry. We decided to give it a try. Our first Sunday there was a shocker. I loved the praise and worship. It reminded me of my private worship time at home, and it drew me into that place of intimacy with the Lord. We were in the second row, and I was excited that no one was sitting in front of us - that meant there would be no distractions while the pastor was teaching. I had come a long way, but I still struggled somewhat to comprehend when others were speaking.

When the praise and worship ended, two people from the platform sat in the empty seats in front of us. The pastor prayed, and then told people to turn and greet those around them. The woman who sat in front of me, a very pretty, short blonde woman, turned and hugged me with eager enthusiasm and said with a bubbly southern accent, "I'm so glad you're here!"

I wanted to run! This woman and her husband, Willard and Teresa McCain, headed the worship department. I hardly heard a word the pastor spoke that day - all I could think about was this woman. I'd been a Christian for almost two years now and I had never seen anyone that excited about life. Something wasn't right in this place. Maybe it was a cult. I wanted to leave.

When the service ended and we were leaving, Mike started talking about how much he loved this church. I was flabbergasted. JR was upset because he wasn't crazy about it either. I tried to explain to Mike that I thought maybe it was a cult, but he wouldn't believe it. This was the first time I'd heard any pastor teach on the grace of God - was it right? We had been hearing preaching about guilt and condemnation. This sounded too good, too nice - and it was free, he had said. What about the punishment for our sins?

We continued to attend, and Teresa approached me regularly, but many times I ran away from her. This woman was full of joy and kindness, and I was sure she was a good person. But if she

76

knew the life I'd lived she wouldn't approach me at all. She would be like the others who found my old life too much to handle. Yet even when I ran from her, I was drawn to her. I watched her from a distance, especially when she was with her husband. She was far different than other women I'd known both in and out of the church.

One day I realized, "I think she *likes* her husband." This was a completely foreign idea to me. They both were extraordinary people. When I was around them, I felt like a life that mattered. They didn't treat me any differently than others. Of course I thought it was because they didn't know the real me and what I had done in my life.

After much encouragement from a lady at church, I decided to go back to business school. I struggled with this decision, because in my heart I wanted to be at home with my children, to be a real mom to them after so many wasted years. But times had changed, and women were supposed to be useful members of society. This was my chance to change things for the better.

I went to Trend Business College in downtown Spokane, and I graduated with honors: a 4.0 GPA and perfect attendance. What a change. I knew I had proved the doctors wrong about my brain cells – God had truly healed and restored my brain. But earning that diploma felt like an empty success to me. I stood on the porch that evening looking at the stars and I asked God, "Is this really important?"

77

I still longed for an old-fashioned lifestyle, to be a wife and mother full-time.

My son JR had moved out this year. He ran away a few times and I brought him home, but he didn't want to be there with us. So he went to stay with his aunt on the reservation, about an hour's drive away.

I began working at the Business College. They hired me as Office Manager, and I filled in for the Dean of Students during an interim. I really enjoyed creating the students' classes, and I was good at it. It was rewarding to get to know each student personally.

Eventually I was hired full-time at a local waste management company, with good pay and benefits. I was doing great on my job, but personally I was still struggling. When I went to see the doctor, he told me I had a chemical imbalance as a result of the years of drug abuse, and he put me on antidepressants. After this I completely shut down emotionally. I went through the motions of life each day, existing, but not feeling anything.

I stood watching my children outside in the yard one day when I saw my 4-year-old daughter fall out of a tree. She was crying hard, but I didn't move an inch. I stood there numb, just staring. Her brother helped her, and eventually I tried to comfort her, but without any emotion. I was missing life, and I felt like I was in a prison all over again.

A few weeks later as I was driving JR back to the reservation, I was pulled over by the police. They told me to slow down and take it easy, and then let me go. But I had a sick feeling inside that something was wrong. Within moments the police car's lights were back on and the siren was blaring. They took me out of the car and cuffed me very cautiously. They had learned of an outstanding warrant for my arrest, and it was noted that I had been very violent while being arrested in the past.

My face was on the trunk of my car, and I could see my children inside crying and scared. Would the past ever be the past in my life? My old instincts to fight back rose up as they were cuffing me, but a voice inside me said *stop*, so I did, and I went peacefully. Meanwhile the police department contacted Mike's work. They talked to his supervisor first and told him what had happened – how humiliating for Mike.

The old familiar sound of cell doors shutting - how did I get back to this place? I knew how. It was the antidepressants. I was no longer making Christ the center of my life, because I was too numb to seek Him while on the meds. I had moved away from Him. *How can I get back, God?*

Mike arrived to pick me up, but instead of going home I continued on to the reservation. That night, for the first time in a long time, I got high; but it wasn't like any high I'd ever experienced. It was tormenting. I saw things I had never seen before, as if I was looking into the spiritual realm of the demonic.

I looked in the mirror and I saw things that I don't know how to describe clinging to me. Instantly I knew what each one of them represented. They were the faces of my old friends, the voices that had lived in me, guided me and taught me all those years. Hate, anger, jealousy, fear, insecurity, manipulation, depression, bitterness, deception, judgment, criticism, suicide, seduction, perversion, lust - and the list went on. I was looking at everything that had controlled my life, and it was ugly. *I want out God! I want out of the past. How do I go forward?*

CHAPTER 14

Later that week when I was at work, my boss came to my desk and told me there was a personal phone call he wanted me to take. Personal calls were normally forbidden. When I asked him who it was, he told me it was a woman from my church, and he didn't know why but he felt I needed to talk to her.

I've never forgotten that telephone call: *"Jay, it's Teresa. Please don't be angry, but Kevin told us about you going to jail. I know about the antidepressants too."* Then she began to speak the Word of God over me, and she encouraged me to choose life instead of death. Toward the end of the call she told me to do something that she would never normally recommend to someone - throw away the antidepressants now. Peace flooded through me and I knew it was the right thing to do. And I did.

Even though I didn't pursue a personal relationship with Teresa McCain, I had continued to watch her and Willard very closely. I noticed so many different things about them, but what stood out most consistently was this: Their lives were about God, and they were living what I was reading in the Word. They were Imitators of Christ.

Imitators! That clicked big time inside of me. As I looked back over my life, I knew that was exactly what I had been - an imitator. I could change masks

81

faster than the average chameleon. I had always been able to adapt immediately to my surroundings: native, biker, cowgirl, stripper, street walker, etc. It didn't matter to what extreme. I had immersed myself in the culture or lifestyle I was in. This had been my survival mode.

Just as a person looks in their closet to decide what clothes to wear, I would look in my closet of masks and ask, "Who should I be today?" Although usually the question was, "Who do I *need* to be today?" On this day I made a heart choice: I wanted to be an imitator of Christ.

Within days of quitting the antidepressants I felt life stirring inside of me again. I was reading the Word again, and I found it helpful to read it out loud to myself. I bought a book called *Prayers That Avail Much* that I overheard Teresa recommend to someone. She mentioned the personal confessions, so I read those out loud every morning and every night. I had a strong desire to really know the word of God and live it out. I wanted to show my husband, children and others that I had changed and become a new person.

A new sense of hope was building in me. I felt like God was telling me that true emotional healing was going to take place. I went forward for prayer one service during an altar call. The woman who prayed for me spoke this word over me: "God has called you to be an integral part of this body of Christ." I was sure she'd made a mistake and given that word to the wrong person, but I didn't want to hurt her feelings. Then another lady prayed over me, and she started thanking God for bringing me into the church office to work. I left that night thinking, *"What is it with these people - do they really hear from God?"*

That was in May of 1991. In June I gave my two-week notice at my job. Almost exactly a month from when those women had prayed over me, I began working at the church office. My boss contended that I was his best employee, and he couldn't understand why I would leave a good paying job for a volunteer position. Honestly, neither could I.

One day while I was typing a letter, I heard music coming from the sanctuary. I walked just inside the doors and saw that it was Willard McCain. He was worshipping alone. I felt like I was intruding on something very private so I stepped back into the doorway, but I couldn't leave. Something strange was happening inside me as I listened to him play and sing.

Memories of all the abuses in my life were flooding to the surface. My heart was racing and I could hardly breathe. *Oh, my God, please help me! I don't want to remember these things anymore!* Suddenly I felt covered with peace, like warm oil was poured over my head. Then an indescribable voice, "I will bind up the brokenhearted. I will breathe life into my child and you will be trained up in the way you should go. Your heart will be strong and filled

with My Word. Trust me. Just trust me and believe."
I knew I had to go write this down.

Then I walked back to the sanctuary, and this vision came to me as I watched Willard: *This is my spiritual father. He will train me up in the things of God. He will teach me how to live for Christ. He will not harm me in any way.* At that point I realized something about Willard that I hadn't been able to identify before: Unlike almost every other man I had ever met, he was not sexually perverted in any way. He was a human example of Christ's pure love. Christ's love is not self-seeking, and neither was Willard or Teresa's.

Many other days followed when I sat in that doorway, praying and worshipping in tears as Willard worshipped at the piano. My scars were deep, but God was beginning to work out a healing in me that was deeper still.

CHAPTER 15

Throughout the next four years I did go through a lot of training up, and I didn't always like it. Living a life devoted to Christ wasn't easy. I experienced the loss of many friendships, and relationships with family members too. Spending much time in prayer and tears, I tried to accept the fact that I will never understand everything in life.

During this time our marriage was still struggling, always a sense of secrecy, and I hated secrets. There was never a time when the family was truly connected. I didn't know what to do to change what was happening. I kept thinking, *my children are growing up and I'll never have this time with them again*. How could I make us a real family, like the ones on The Walton's and Little House on the Prairie?

The church was going through a struggle at this time too. Many people were verbally attacking and judging one another. It was like watching vultures turn on each other. Such a harsh time, yet God kept telling me to keep my eyes on Him and to speak only life and love.

In September 1993 I was praying when I saw this vision:

Ocean waves were crashing against the shore, mostly small at the beginning. But key people were leaving with each wave. Then a huge wave came in, and with it were many new faces of people coming into the church. God said they would come in differently than before, and they would be involved in ministry that would reach out into the community. They would be impacting this community for Christ.

Somehow I knew that the pastor would also go out with that wave. This vision confused me. If the wave took away the pastor, who was going to lead the church? I told Willard about it, and he told me to write it down and date it, so I did.

A few weeks later God directed Willard and Teresa to return home to Missouri. This was painful for me, but they had trained me well. I thanked God for the time I'd had with them, and I knew that my eyes were not to be focused on people but on God.

In December our pastor resigned, and Willard returned to help bring in a new pastor. But God also called Willard and Teresa back to Spokane, and they resumed their position as worship leaders. God had revealed to me that He was calling Willard to pastor this church body. As I was talking with him in my office one day, I shared this with him. It was the first time he ever raised his voice at me in anger. He had no desire to be a pastor, he was a worship leader, and he let me know that very clearly. Amazingly, I didn't take his anger personally as a rejection. Why was that? I normally did when people spoke to me that way.

After this time of upheaval in our church, our new pastor brought healing and restoration. The joy of the Lord was filling our church body, something we hadn't had before.

A new member of the staff was continually encouraging me in the work I did in the finance office, but he also pointed out that I was not valued by the others. I was their work horse - not someone they spent time with in public, but someone they used for their own benefit. Whoosh – after hearing these comments several times, the flashbacks came in like a flood:

> *Men in the dark using me to bring them pleasure... A mother who was embarrassed to be seen in public with me, who couldn't bring herself to even hug me... Everyone enjoying me in the secret hidden dark places, but never in public... I brought shame on everyone because I was damaged goods...*

Before long my perception of those around me was being distorted by suspicion.

In the summer of 1995 I resigned from the church staff. I wanted to go home and allow God to complete the healing inside of me. I needed to escape the judgment I felt, and I didn't want to be an embarrassment to WIllard and the pastor.

Within a month Mike and I got involved in a Christian biker ministry. I believed this was a great area for me to minister to others since it was a part of my past lifestyle, but I didn't spend time in prayer about it first.

I began to change a lot. Depression set in and I was fighting it hard, but I didn't allow others to know the turmoil going on inside me. As I entered a store one day, I opened the door for an elderly woman who was coming out. When she looked at me I saw fear and uncertainty on her face, and a warning bell sounded within me. I used to enjoy seeing fear in people's eyes, but that was the old Jaylene. Now I felt sad and ashamed that I would affect another life this way.

I went home and looked at myself in the mirror. My hair was very, very dark, I was dressed in all black, and there was *no life* in my eyes. I had drifted away, no, walked away from God's will for my life. How did this happen so easily? I was trying to serve God "my way" and it wasn't working. I asked God to help me get back to where I belonged with Him.

Mike and I made a weekend trip to our home town to get away, talk, and make some decisions. Things were still strained in our marriage; I kept sensing there were secrets. As I sat in the park watching the people, the phrase "people need the Lord" sounded repeatedly in my mind. Mike and I discussed the possibility of moving "home" to start over, and to minister to the people there.

Several months later we made the decision to move. Our current pastor asked to meet with us over lunch before we left. The Lord had given him a word of warning for us: "Mike, the enemy has established a snare for you. Jaylene, you need to intercede for him stronger than you ever have." I asked if the Lord had shown him whether we should go, but he didn't know. Another man in the church spoke very boldly to Mike and me and told us that it was not God's will for us to make this move.

I didn't have peace about it, but we made the move anyway. One of the hardest changes was that there wasn't a strong church to attend. We did begin attending a church regularly, but the Word of God was not really being taught - it was more of a social gathering. However I was grateful for the fellowship with other believers. Eventually the pastor asked me to help with their books at the church. I told him I wasn't interested. He asked again, and again I said no; but then he asked if I would just look and give them some suggestions. I agreed, and the next thing I knew I was serving in the church office.

CHAPTER 16

Within two weeks of leaving Spokane I knew without a doubt this move was not God's will, as I watched what was left of my family begin to fall apart. All of my life I'd had one dream, to be a part of a family. Now the closest I had ever been to it was dissolving before my eyes, and I was powerless to stop it.

I went to God in prayer and sought his forgiveness and direction. I recognized that this was a pattern I'd lived out many times before. Whenever I did things in my own understanding, I ended up in a mess. Then I cried out to God to save me, and in His mercy and grace God would forgive me and help me. But this time I knew inside I was going to learn something very valuable.

Not long after we moved, our son left home. He had begun using drugs and drinking heavily, and his time had come to break away from the family. About the same time, it was exposed that Mike was using his workplace computers for pornography and that he was involved in multiple adulterous relationships. He lost his job, and word spread quickly through the community.

As my husband told me about all of the things he had done and the women he'd been involved with, I could barely breathe. My head was spinning, my stomach turned and I felt like I was falling into a deep, dark pit. How could this happen? I had interceded more than ever before for my marriage. I had sought God with my whole heart and committed to living my life as He led me.

This triggered an even deeper source of pain inside me – the many years of abuse and rapes that occurred in my life had happened in this very town. Now, years later, this town was destroying my life again. That was how I saw it. I didn't recognize that the real root of the situation was spiritual.

As I was praying that evening, a vision appeared before me of a large hand - I knew immediately it was God's hand. He was pulling it up out of a muddy black pit, and in his hand was my husband. I heard very clearly, almost in an audible voice, "I am creating a new man. Love him unconditionally, and do not turn him away." Now I felt sick. I felt like God cared nothing about my feelings of pain or about protecting me, just like an earthly abusive parent. It was just about pleasing and protecting the man again. That's what it had always been about.

I offered my husband his freedom. However, he insisted it wasn't what he wanted. We went to our pastor's home, but he told us he didn't know what to do for us. Once again the church did not know how to deal with my life.

The worst part of this ordeal was not that I was hurting, but my daughter's pain. Our daughter Carly was twelve during this time, and life hit her hard. She went to school one morning not knowing about anything that had happened, and none of her friends would have anything to do with her. Everyone knew what her daddy had done - parents had obviously been talking about it in their homes. She paid a price for her father's sins. My daughter was suffering deeply, and I was unable to help her. She was left to learn on her own how to survive. She never should have had to experience any of this. She was dying inside, and I was nearly dead. I had nothing to offer her, no way to help her... she experienced complete abandonment.

We drove to Spokane to see Willard (who was now the pastor!) and Teresa. They saw us as they pulled into the church parking lot and stopped the car to talk to us. Teresa looked at me and knew right away something was very wrong. We told them we needed to see them, and they made arrangements to meet right then.

It was a very intense, emotionally painful meeting. Pastor Willard was literally a couple inches from Mike's face as he confronted him not just about what had occurred recently, but also about things he had confronted him on before we ever left. He also described very graphically to Mike the condition of my heart. I felt like I was going to break down unless I found a solid anchor to focus on, so I turned to Teresa, knowing she would be strong and composed. But tears were falling down her face, and the pain in her eyes revealed another facet of this mighty woman of God: love and compassion. There was no way for me to avoid this pain. Yet at the same time, I had never experienced such love and caring. Even as pastor confronted Mike, he did it with a love that amazed me.

We returned home and worked at the healing process. Every week we drove to Spokane to attend an MMI (Marriage Ministries International) meeting. These meetings were difficult. The pain I lived in was so raw, and to sit in a teaching class just didn't help me with living. We did this for 13 weeks, and at home we also attended Cleansing Stream ministry meetings. We were being saturated in the Word of God.

I still felt a lack of trust in God, and my fear of not being taken care of or protected was very deep. So when Mike was unable to get work, I began using my church credit card to pay for food, gas and utilities. I knew how wrong it was, but fear won the battle within me. Once again I was leaning on my own understanding to do things my way. I was also acting out of pride - I told myself that this town had done nothing but destroy me since before I was born, and I was not going to allow it the honor of making me homeless too. I was fighting the wrong enemy but I didn't know it.

The current events were not all that was tormenting me. Everything I hadn't dealt with from my old life now surfaced, and I was treading water in a sea of demons. They were all there: the visions of every rape, beating, and molestation; my own sinful acts of sexual addictions; child abuse; hate; and anger. It was all so vivid and suffocating. I don't know any other way to describe it.

My desire to survive was gone. Eventually I went to the deepest level of depression I'd ever experienced. I was essentially paralyzed - I could no longer speak, think, or move. Having absolutely no hope for any good in my life, I prayed hard for death to come quickly. But it didn't - the torment continued. An old friend visited me, a voice I recognized instantly, and he was laughing at what my belief in God had brought me to. What a fool I had been.

In the bathtub one evening, I felt so very close to death. I craved it desperately, pleading for it to come. I knew it had to come. Then Mike entered the bathroom and held the phone to my ear. On the other end was Dawn from our church in Spokane. She was speaking the word of God and praying for new life to enter my heart. She was warring for me. Why would someone fight for my life? There was no value to it, no purpose for it - the truth of that had been shown to me time and again. But as she kept praying, something in me stirred. I began to believe something - I'm not sure what - but life was sparking inside of me.

Now I could see I was facing a choice. Would I continue to choose death, allowing Satan to have the victory over my life? Or would I choose life, believing that I am who God says I am, and that who the Son sets free, is free indeed? I could choose to walk a life of faith in Christ no matter what life might deal me, or I could choose to give up every time I was hit. The Word of God came rushing back in, flooding me with His love and peace. It was drawing me to Him once again. I chose life!

In my mind I saw this visual of the prison I had lived in, and I drew it on paper. Each bar of the prison cell represented something that had a hold on me, lies that had been a part of my life for as long as I could remember.

- ⇒ Unwanted
- ⇒ Unloved
- ⇒ Abandonment
- ⇒ Abuse
- ⇒ Rejection
- ⇒ Hate/Anger
- ⇒ Insecurities
- ⇒ Shame
- ⇒ Failure
- ⇒ Fear
- ⇒ Worthless
- ⇒ Depression
- ⇒ Unbelief
- ⇒ Selfish
- ⇒ Lonely
- ⇒ Never chosen

"Okay, God," I prayed, "if this is ever going to change, I need you to show me some sign that there is going to be life again; not existence, but real life."

Not long after that we developed a relationship with our son Andy's ex-girlfriend, who was pregnant with his child. On July 29, 1998, I was in that delivery room with her as she gave birth to my first grandchild, Tony. God's sign of confirmation was right before my eyes. When he was born and the doctor lifted him up to us, my mind raced back to nearly 18 years ago when his dad had been born. He looked just like Andy. It was amazing - it was life.

My heart was filled with God's love for this baby, and most of all for Him. My grandson Tony was used by God so much that first year to encourage and heal my heart. "My God, you are so good and faithful. Guard and protect this child. He will grow to be a mighty warrior in Christ." That was my prayer for this beautiful child.

CHAPTER 17

On May 30, 1999, my second grandchild was born, and I was there for his birth also. He was born in the same hospital his father was born in. This was JR's first child, and he was born 23 years to the day that JR had been taken from me. This meant nothing to anyone else, but it meant everything to me. God had blessed me with another beautiful grandchild, and this one had his Grandma Jay's eyes! "Lord, let his eyes seek You, and let him serve You with his whole heart." That was my prayer as I held him and cried.

New life was springing up around me, but God loves us too much to allow us to continue in our sins. He wants life for us, and soon my own sin of using the church credit card was exposed. I was horribly ashamed, but relieved at the same time. I had spent close to $2000 over the past year, but the church allowed me to make payments on it. God provided the money for all that I owed, except for the portion of Mike's debt on the card for a computer he had purchased. I never disclosed his part of it; I left that to God to take care of.

Even after that exposure, God placed me in a position of leadership in the Women's Ministry to lead the women's retreat. I was amazed. After what I had done, how could He use me? As I planned and prepared for that retreat, new life was emerging within me. My relationship with Christ wasn't anything like it had been before - it was even better and stronger. The retreat was phenomenal. Lives were touched and changed for the good, and so was I.

The following year I led another retreat, and while I was gone a man came to town looking for me. He met with my husband and explained that he was my uncle, my biological father's half-brother. He recently found out about me, and put together a photo album for me of my father's life and other family members. When I returned, Mike shared what had happened and told me he felt I should be alone to look at the album. I thought, *"How ridiculous. I don't even know the people - they have no emotional meaning to me."*

Mike left, and I picked up the album. In the front was a large senior picture of my dad, the only one I had ever seen of him because it was hung up in the high school. When I turned to the next page, it was filled with pictures of him as a small child, in chronological order, and it took my breath away. I continued to turn pages and watched him grow before my eyes. For the first time in my life I saw a visual fit for myself - I could have been my father's twin. Throughout every stage I looked identical to him.

Overcome with anguish, I fell to the floor in gut-wrenching screams. To this day I cannot fully describe the many emotions I experienced in that moment, but what it boiled down to was loss. He could have been the first person who would have actually loved and accepted me. Yet I didn't know him. Maybe he would have wanted me and protected me. All the maybes in the world were not going to change the facts: he was dead, and I would never know him or the truth of who I was to him.

Then the truth from God's Word rose up inside me: Jesus is the Way, the Truth, and the Life, and He had always loved me and wanted me. *"Lord God, help me to walk this journey out. I don't know why this has come into my life at this time, but You do. Show me Your way."*

When I eventually contacted my uncle, he told me that I have a half-sister and asked if I wanted to contact her. I knew I wasn't ready for this step, but I got her email address. I waited a long time before contacting her, but time didn't make it any easier to take that step, it just allowed fear and doubt to grow.

When I did make contact, I was amazed at our similarities. Not in appearance, because I hadn't seen any pictures of her, but in our attitudes and ways of thinking. She had been abandoned by her mother when our dad died, when she was only a year old. Our grandmother legally adopted her and raised her up as her own. She eventually met her mother and the family, but they were very dysfunctional. She had no desire to develop a relationship with them or to have her children around them.

Within a month after the women's retreat, the Lord told me it was time to leave. I struggled with resigning from my work at the church, and tried to understand it in the natural. Financially it made no sense to do such a thing. I couldn't figure it out, but God had a plan.

Soon we were driving to Spokane every Sunday to attend church at Grace Harvest again. It was wonderful and refreshing - it was home. Within a matter of weeks, Mike and I both had full-time jobs in Spokane along with a place to live. During my prayer time I kept sensing, "Now's the time. Get ready." Get ready for what?

CHAPTER 18

Less than a year later it began... the hardest battle of my marriage. I turned on the shower one morning while I was getting ready for work. As I began to step in, I had this strong thought, "Go into the living room". It was so compelling that I didn't question it. I walked out to discover my husband at the computer in the middle of a cyber-sex act. It was sickening. I couldn't even get words out, and I hit him so hard it knocked him to the floor. I turned and went to the shower. I felt sick and dirty, and no matter how hard I scrubbed I could not get clean. Would there ever be a time in my life when that dirty feeling could not take hold of me?

I began thinking about my marriage. I told God, "He has to go. I don't want him here anymore." Then as I prayed, once again the Lord spoke to my heart, "Love him, Jaylene. Just love him. Speak the truth in love and trust me to do the work." My mind said, "No, this is sick!" I went to Mike and told him he had choices to make, and now, because he was about to lose everything. Then I left for work, shaking, sick, and overwhelmed with pain.

The revelation of what Mike was into kept increasing for several days. Every time I turned on the computer, something else was before my eyes - women exposing themselves. It was disgustingly sick. One woman thought I was Mike on the instant messenger, and she started talking to him very graphically about sexual things she wanted to do to him. Danger! I felt it, the stirrings as she was talking. Oh no, it was that old sick stuff rousing inside of me, drawing me. Shut it off!

The next time I went online a web cam video of a woman came on, and all of the old sexual desires awakened as she went through each familiar act on camera. The things she said to me, as she thought it was my husband, stirred it up stronger and stronger. It was my old friends, pornography and seduction. I began to coach her into doing multiple things to her body. I was not even "there" at the moment; I went with it so quickly and naturally. It was all coming back, powerful and destructive.

Suddenly I realized what was happening. I was frozen, and sick. I could see the desperation which drove her. She was willing to do anything and everything to satisfy the maddening torture of the cravings in her body. I remembered those feelings and knew that she would give up everything while lost in that moment. "Oh, my God, what have I done? Help me! Help her! Please not again, I can't go back! Daddy, I need you to save me from myself!"

I almost threw that computer across the room. I wanted a sledgehammer to destroy it, anything to make it stop. But the problem wasn't the computer. "For our struggle is not against flesh and blood …but against the powers of this dark world and against the spiritual forces of evil in the heavenly realms." (Eph 6:12) The problem was the spirit that was operating in and through this woman and me.

I fell on my face and screamed out to God to cleanse me, asking how and why I could have done such a thing after all these years of freedom. I realized even more how important it is to guard my mind and my heart. I could be back into everything I had come out of - just one choice made in a split second could destroy my whole life and those around me.

Mike decided to get help, and he began meeting with an associate pastor at our church. For a while he diligently tried to keep things right, but then he fell back into it again.

A few years later, Mike's boss scheduled a meeting with him. On the day of the meeting as we were preparing for work I said, "Let's pray before we leave this morning." I prayed that God would reveal everything that was hidden, anything that could harm us in any way. Mike later said that as I was praying he knew without a doubt it was going to happen, all of his hidden secrets were about to be exposed.

An hour after I arrived at work, he came to see me. He had just lost his job because he'd been having an emotional affair with a woman for over a year. There had been a few sexual acts in the beginning, but then it shifted to constant phone calls throughout the day and night - phone calls on the company's cell phone. It was another form of addiction. This was it for me. I was done with the whole thing.

103

For the first time I sensed a release from God to move forward with or without Mike in my life. Mike was desperate to keep the marriage together, but I wasn't interested. He called the woman he'd been involved with and reached her voice mail. I listened as he left her a message, and specifically said, "I choose my wife; our relationship is over."

I tried to contact her as well, unsuccessfully. So I called her home and spoke to her husband. He had suspected something was happening after seeing them together at a fast food place. Everything broke loose after that, and she called to apologize to me. Then she spoke to Mike and told him to never contact her again.

Pastor Willard called me that night. After we talked for a bit he said, "Jay, I'm not concerned about you, because I know that you'll come out of this standing. But I am worried about Mike. You know I never encourage anyone in divorce, but if anyone has spiritual and natural grounds for one, you do. Teresa and I are with you whatever you decide." I knew right then and there the answer, and I said, "There won't be a divorce."

How could I say that? What was I thinking? I felt betrayed even by myself at that point. I questioned every little thing about my decision. Was this because of all those years of being trained to protect my abusers? Was it because I didn't think anyone else would ever want me? Was I afraid of being alone? Was I addicted to bad behavior?

As I was praying, a question came to me: "What is the worst thing that could ever happen to you?" I knew the answer right away: "To not have God in my life." And then I had peace. I knew that God would never leave me or forsake me – I would always have him in my life. And with his help I could handle whatever else came my way.

I knew what I needed to do next. I told Mike he had to leave, and ironically, it was hard for me to do. Even though it was what I wanted, it was very painful. That night Mike and I both had very intense spiritual dreams.

Jaylene's dream:

> I saw Mike sitting at the head of a long table, like a huge banquet table, with many people seated there. But he was different - there was a peacefulness and joy about him. Then I heard a voice saying, "I will prepare a table before you in the presence of your enemies; I will anoint your head with oil; your cup runs over."

Mike's dream:

> He saw a man laying face down on the ground, but only half of him could be seen, because he was so deep down in the dirt. He looked like a shell instead of an actual living person. Then he heard a voice that said, "Lay

your hands on him and pray for life in the dead places." As he began to pray he could see life entering the man, and he began to rise up out of the ground. When the man stood before him, he saw that it was himself.

After dreams like that, it was natural for me to doubt that I was to send him away. But somehow I knew that I had to follow through.

My friend Kim came to town to stay that night with me. As Mike was leaving that afternoon, we were both in tears. Kim even questioned whether it was right to send him out. My only response was, "Shut up and pray." I began to pray for a complete breaking, a crushing, to take place in Mike's life, to the point where there would be nothing left of himself to rely on; that he would commit himself to God like never before; and that every back door of his life would be shut permanently.

Kim cried even harder. She felt I was being too harsh. But I wasn't being cruel - I was fighting for a man's life. I didn't know if he would ever be a part of my life again, but I wanted his life to be right with God. I wanted him to truly experience life for the first time. All he had ever known was the bondage and darkness of his addictions, and the masks he wore to impress women. He had never really been himself with anyone, for fear of rejection. I wanted this man to be free to live, to be free from all of the sick things I had helped bring into his life. The warrior in Christ had arisen in me!

Mike received an offer to stay at a woman's house that night, but he chose to stay in his car in the Wal-Mart parking lot. God's work had begun, and it was a grueling night for him. By morning Mike had undeniably been crushed, as he cried out to God to save him from himself. He went to the river and buried everything that he had received from the women he'd been involved with. Then he made a commitment to God to live for Him completely, and he gave God permission to begin working in his life. Mike came home that same day - and really I think he was coming home for the very first time.

Not long after this, I overheard a group of people talking about Mike and me, and about the sins that had been exposed in his life. Several people I knew quit associating with me completely, not even a hello. Although I was deeply hurt, God brought me through it victoriously. I was learning that I needed to be where He wanted me to be, regardless of what people were saying or doing. The rejection was painful, but I found security in knowing that I am valuable to God. We all are.

Just two months after Mike committed his life to the Lord, my half-sister came to Washington, along with my biological grandmother. It was time to meet. *Can I do this, God?* During the two-hour drive to where they were, I was in turmoil. But as I prayed, God told me this: "Their acceptance or rejection of you will not affect who you are, Jaylene, or what I have in your future. It is of no eternal value." Once again I had peace, His peace.

I met most of the family, and they were all wonderful. When my grandma was told who I was (she had just turned 90 years old), she rose up off the couch and embraced me, saying, "I never called you back. I'm so sorry." No one else in that room knew except her and me what that meant, but God did, and He knew what I needed to hear.

I love my grandmother. She was recently moved to California and I don't have the contact with her that I did for that short period of time, but I will spend eternity with her, and my father... my real Father, my Heavenly Father.

You see, what I always thought was so important - finding my biological family, knowing them, being wanted and accepted by them - still did not fill that empty place in my heart. Only God could, because it's a place that was created by Him and for Him alone. All my life I had tried to fill that place inside me that desired "something more" with the wrong things: sex, drugs, alcohol, things, people, and so much more. But only God was sufficient to fill it. I have learned that He is more than enough to meet every need I have.

That was six years ago. Mike was not changed overnight; no one is. But he has faithfully sought God every day of his life since then. And I know he will continue to do so.

The healing in our marriage took a lot of time. So much damage had been done by both of us. It wasn't just Mike's mistakes that had brought us to this point. I laid a foundation of unfaithfulness, mistrust, and fear; probably more than I realize even now. I'm not excusing Mike's actions - I'm just being honest and looking at the whole picture.

Mike and I found that to overcome our brokenness and reconnect, we *had* to have the Father. Does that sound weak and foolish to you? Here is my formula for how we overcame:

F = Forgiveness is needed in order for you to move on. Not "amnesia", but choosing to forgive and move forward. This is something you have to make the decision to do continuously, everyday - and you need God's help to do it.

A = Accountability and attitude adjustments are needed regularly! Anger and bitterness will set in if you do not control it by continuing to forgive.

T = Trust. I had to always place my trust in God, not in my husband or friends. Trust God, and allow Him to begin to change your heart.

H = Honesty - being completely open, regardless of how invading or foolish It may seem. This is where accountability comes in also... do not attempt to "hide" anything.

E = Endure: to remain firm under suffering or misfortune without yielding *(Webster's Dictionary).* You must push through the painful stages you will experience on this journey.

R = Respect for each other is a must. Don't confuse this with "earning" one another's respect. You must make a decision to respect each other as human beings; it is so tempting to treat each other as worthless scum during this time. Respect and love go hand in hand. This is not a *feeling*, but a *choice* of your actions and attitude.

You need the "FATHER" to get through to the place of healing and victory. F-A-T-H-E-R and all that it stands for are based on God and His Word.

Today, Mike and I do trust each other, and we are best friends. We are human of course, and still have moments when life hits and we may doubt or struggle with temptation. Sometimes things come up that connect us to a painful memory. It's up to us to let each other know – we know that if we attempt to keep anything a secret we will be in trouble again. We also have to remind ourselves that those things are in the past. The mind is a powerful thing and it can destroy the most beautiful relationships if we don't keep our perspectives healthy and believe the truth. Don't allow suspicions to destroy you.

CHAPTER 19

I wasn't changed overnight, either. I had a lot of extreme issues to overcome, and that doesn't happen quickly. It literally took years to overcome the masturbation and the old ways of thinking. I worked hard to retrain my mind to see people as human beings, not sexual beings. I spent years struggling with all of the sexual addictions, overcoming through the Word of God – spending time reading the Bible, learning what God's Word says about life, about Him, and most of all about who I am in Christ. And I am overcoming more and more every day.

So many times in my life before I was saved, I wanted to change myself and make my life into something good, but my attempts always failed. What I didn't know then is that I was powerless to change myself. I needed to *be changed*, to allow God to change me from the inside out. When I allowed Him to enter in, He made changes in my heart, and those changes on the inside of me started to effect changes in how I lived. That doesn't mean it's always been easy; living the life of a Christ Follower is far from easy. I've had to cooperate with God and the work He's doing in me – that's why change "takes work" – but it's a work I can only do with His strength. When I try to work change with my own strength, I fail.

111

People always ask: If God is real, then why did He let those horrible things happen to you? Why are there wars? Why is there sickness and suffering? Who wants to serve a God who allows that kind of cruelty?

The answer is: I do! Because I know the hell that I lived in, I know the depth of torturous pain that I endured mentally, physically & emotionally. But when I met Jesus at that altar, for the first time I experienced peace and healing. I met love at that altar, a pure love that I didn't know existed, and I received life.

Every choice we make in life has a result, either good or bad, and it always affects others. We tend to believe the lie that our wrong choices hurt only ourselves; often they hurt more than we can imagine. So, what if there was no God? Who would we blame for all of the pain and suffering in life? Would it make every evil thing that happens more acceptable? Really, how would it change our perspective about what happens in life?

I know that bad things happen to everyone, regardless of their beliefs. But I also know that there is one true God who wants to love, comfort and help us through each step we take in this life. Many of us will experience a variety of hardships, but it doesn't mean that God is cruel, weak, or not real. It means that we can walk through the journey of life and continue to grow stronger through each trial, believe deeper through each victory. And hopefully we will reach outside of ourselves to others, and help them to believe and continue on to that place of victory in their lives also.

Visualize an elderberry tree that has been neglected: it's full of tall, twisted branches that have intertwined with each other, but as spring approaches new branches spring up in various places. Those branches can either begin to grow with new life and produce fruit, or they can die off like the others before summer even sets in. The tree needs water, sunshine and some tender care.

That's how the human life is. It's how my life was; in the midst of all the dead places in my life, some form of new life was always trying to reach me. The only way new life can take root inside of us is if we have hope. Without hope there is no life; we continue to grow sick and depressed. Then another layer of hardness surrounds our heart. Eventually life will try to reach in again; however, it is always a choice whether we choose life or death.

One thing we must do is change our focus! Focus outward instead of on yourself; don't continuously look at everything you see wrong with yourself and your circumstances. Start by finding at least one thing each day that you can be thankful for, whether it's your health, your eyesight, or the fact that you can walk. You can find at least one thing. It's a starting place, and each day you will begin to see more options in life. There is always hope, but the only true hope is in Christ.

113

As an adult I learned some information about my family history that helped me to understand why things happened in my life the way they did.

My great grandmother:

One day her father left for the day and never returned, leaving them somewhere in Montana. He left without ever saying goodbye. He went to Texas and started a whole new family - new wife, new children - never once returning to his first wife and children, never communicating with them in any way, not even to let them know that he was still alive.

She was molested as a child, and she was taught that ladies never speak of such things. She was a survivor; she became strong and resilient to the hardships in life. But she also loved her children, grandchildren, and many great-grandchildren. She was resourceful and wise. She was my gram.

My grandmother:

She had four children, and one day she left them alone in a motel room to go and begin a new life for herself. But a day or two later she returned to take two of them with her, my mom and one of her brothers, leaving the oldest and youngest behind. She went to California, traveled with the carnival, and lived a life that was completely irresponsible, never taking care of her children.

One day when she was off someplace with a man, my mom's brother was killed by some neighborhood boys who put him in a burning barrel. My mother stood by watching as he was burned; she was a small child and was unable to help him. He was hospitalized, but they were unable to save him. Authorities were not even able to locate my grandmother at the time.

My mother:

She grew up in a variety of surroundings, following carnivals, hanging around truckers, and so on. She was sexually molested as a child. She experienced the trauma of seeing her brother murdered. She was alone, abandoned by her mother.

In 1957 she became pregnant with me at the age of 16. She felt like her life was over. Everything would change if she had a child; she wasn't ready for it, nor did she desire it. Her grandmother tried several times to abort the baby, without success. The only other option was to send her away until the baby was born; so, she was returned to her mother (who also did not want the responsibilities of being a parent) in California.

Many of the boys from her hometown were in that area serving in the military. Even though she was pregnant, she began dating one of those boys. In September of 1958 she gave birth to me. Two months later she married this young man, and then returned home without me or her new husband to finish school. During this time she saw my biological father. He wanted to know every detail about me, and then he asked her to marry him. But she was already married – what could she do? What she had wished for could now never be, because of a decision made out of desperation.

When she returned to her new husband in California, she became pregnant again and gave birth to a boy in January of 1960. She became pregnant yet again and had a daughter in February of 1961, giving her three children under the age of three.

Do you see all of the choices that were made by my family that set a foundation for each generation? Abandonment, abuse, rejection, selfishness, worthlessness, and the list just goes on. These traits pass from generation to generation, unless someone breaks it. I am that someone, and I will fight spiritually for each and every one of my descendants.

I choose to see my mother through the eyes of Christ, with compassion and forgiveness. To this day I have never seen my mother truly enjoy life in any way, but I continue to pray for her. I've accepted the fact that in the midst of her own pain, she had no understanding of how to be a mother, or how to love like a mother. She was too lost in her own search for life outside of the pain.

I understand now why she ran away from me when I was burned as a child; I can't imagine what went through her mind and emotions when she saw me screaming and on fire. She must have experienced flashbacks to the memory of her brother being burned, and all the emotions that went along with that. Perhaps she even questioned why it was happening to her child now. I don't know any of the answers, but I do know that she's my mother and I love her.

And didn't I end up the same way in the midst of my own pain, unable to love and care for my child? Who am I to judge her? It's so easy to pass judgment when you're looking at someone's life from the outside, without any understanding of where they've been. "The Lord sees not as man sees; for man looks on the outward appearance, but the Lord looks on the heart." (1 Samuel 16:7)

My heart's desire is for you to know that no matter what you've done, no matter how dark it may be, you matter to God. He doesn't look at you with judgment for the things you've done, as people so often do – He looks at your heart, and He desperately longs to fill that place inside you that only He can fill. No matter what people may say about you, you are beautiful and precious to God. Man's measurement is a lie, but God's view of you is the truth.

The biggest lie Satan uses against us is that we should be fearful of being exposed, of being seen for who we really are – because then we'll be rejected and alone. And so we strive to be who people want us to be. That's just what I did when I looked into my closet of masks each day and asked, "Who should I be today?" Even after I received the Lord, I was sure that if people in the church knew the truth of what I had done, they would condemn me. I lived in fear of pleasing people.

But not anymore! I am so thankful that God loves me for who I am – for who I *really* am. He is the one who created me, and He has always wanted me, even when I wasn't wanted by the family I was born into. Now I try to please *Him* every day of my life, simply by believing Him and loving Him back for who He is.

Today, I no longer have to make believe to see my life as something good. Today, I belong to a family, God's family. I am beautiful, clean and safe. I have a Father who loves me and wants me. I still don't look like the rest of the family, and yes, I am "different", but now I am thankful for that difference - and happy to just be me. I have learned that family is not just biological; many times there are people in our lives whose bond is stronger than blood family.

A few years ago, I discovered something very special about the rock house that I used to play outside of as a child. My biological father had lived there, and that's where he took me for our visits. I don't remember those visits, but my mind connected that house to the things that were lacking in my life: good, safe, clean, love. As a child I felt that the strong rocks of that house would protect me. And ultimately, God used it to lead me to my real protector, my real Father.

> Hear my cry, O God;
> > Attend to my prayer.
> From the end of the earth I will cry to You,
> > When my heart is overwhelmed;
> > Lead me to the **rock** that is higher than I.
>
> For You have been a **shelter** for me,
> > A **strong tower** from the enemy.
> I will abide in Your tabernacle forever;
> > I will trust in the shelter of Your wings.
>
> -Psalm 61:1-4

Recently I received multiple one-word descriptions of myself from others, and the most common word was this: strong. I realize that it's God's strength they see in me. He is my rock, my shelter, my strong tower to protect me from the enemy, and I trust in Him.

Am I perfect? No way! Every day I face a choice to live my life for God, and not to go back into the old lifestyle of bondage. I've learned how crucial it is for me to spiritually guard my mind and heart. If I open the door to sin even just a tiny bit, it gives the enemy opportunity to blow that door wide open. You can't come out of a life of garbage and play both sides of the fence – it's too dangerous. The life I lived before I found Christ was a tormenting prison. But Jesus rescued me and set me free. I choose to stay free.

Jesus said in John 8:32: "And you will know the Truth, and the Truth will set you free." To be set free we need to know the Truth, and the Truth is a person: Jesus Christ, the living Son of God. He died on the cross for my sins, and for your sins, so that we may have eternal life, real life, starting right here and now. That is what it means to be set free, and that's what happened to me when I received him.

Have you allowed Him to set you free? He loves you more than you can *ever* begin to imagine – so much that he was willing to lay down his life to get the key that unlocks your prison cell. There's no sin too great for him to forgive. And there's nothing you can do to make Him stop loving you. All He wants from you is your heart, so that He can fill that empty place in it that longs for Him – and then HE will begin to change you from the inside out. Will you ask Him to come in? There are no magic words to say, simply tell Him that you need Him, and you want Him – invite Jesus to come live in your heart. And He will!

My prayer for you as you finish this book is that you choose life. John 8:36 says, "So if the Son sets you free, you are truly free." I pray that in that freedom you will truly live – not just survive, but live - and experience the freedom to be who God created you to be.

Today, my husband Mike and I minister to marriages that are hurting and desperate, just as ours was. We each also minister to men and women one-on-one, mentoring to "train them up in the way they should go." I enjoy my life to the fullest, and I'm excited about continuing to grow and change every day. I like who I am... I am a daughter of the Lord Most High!

Sharing my story is a *huge* step for me, but it's one I trust Him in. God gave me this revelation to help me deal with my fear of judgment from others as they read about my life:

> As I give myself completely to Him, then "my story" becomes "His Story", and when it is "His Story" it is "history"!

My past is just that now - it is past. Thank you, Jesus.

If you have never accepted Christ and you don't know how or even what to pray, please just talk to Him. There are no special or perfect words to speak; it's just like talking to your best friend. Here is a prayer you can say to accept Christ if you would like:

<u>To Receive Jesus as Your Lord and Savior</u>

> Father,
> You loved the world so much that You gave Your only begotten Son to die for our sins, so that whoever believes in Him will not perish but have eternal life. I don't know if I even know what this means, but I know that I need help, God. I need to know without a doubt that You are real and that You love me, and I need Your forgiveness. Please cleanse me, fill me with Your peace, and just show me how to live. Give me another chance at life, Lord God. I choose at this moment to live completely for You, and to believe in You. In Jesus Name, AMEN!!!

Made in the USA
Columbia, SC
28 April 2023